THE IMPA

Ladies Using Their Infl

By
Chip Baker

Co-authored by Powerful Influencers

2022

Impact
Others ♡

THE
IMPACT

LADIES USING THEIR INFLUENCE

OF

TO CREATE A LIFE OF IMPACT

INFLUENCE

VOLUME 3

WRITTEN BY

CHIP BAKER

CO-AUTHORED BY POWERFUL INFLUENCERS

First Printing: 2022

ISBN: 978-1-7379501-3-4

Ordering Information:

Special discounts are available on quantity purchases by corporations, associations, educators, and others. For details, contact the publisher at the email listed below.

U.S. trade bookstores and wholesalers:
Please contact chipbakertsc@gmail.com.

DEDICATION

This book is dedicated to all of the people who have impacted our lives. We send a special dedication to our families and all of those who support us. We hope that this book will leave an everlasting impact and influence for many generations to come.

We are grateful for you!

PREFACE

Dear reader,

We hope that this book will be a blessing to you. In the following chapters, you will find the lessons that these powerful authors have learned throughout their journey to success. Our hope is that you will learn from these lessons and use them to help you operate more efficiently and effectively in your life.

Brief Description of Book

We all have been impacted by amazing influences in our lives. As such, we create an everlasting ripple effect by learning lessons from those that have affected us. When we apply those lessons, we can make our world a better place.

The Impact of Influence Vol. 3, Ladies Using Their Impact to Create a Life of Influence, is overflowing with wisdom from visionary author Chip Baker and other powerful influencers who have discovered their paths to success. They are influencing many and impacting generations. The inspirational stories within the pages of this book will inspire you to make a positive difference for those around you.

This empowering compilation highlights women that have faced challenges head-on, learned from each of them and pulled the blessings from the lessons. These women are now impacting our world in an amazing way.

TABLE OF CONTENTS

LIST OF AUTHORS IN CHAPTER ORDER

1. Chip Baker
2. Aisha Foy
3. Alecia Thomas
4. Amy Anderson
5. Amy P. Kelly
6. Andrea Bitner
7. Deidre Vasquez
8. Denise Franco
9. Jeni Neatherlin
10. Jennifer A. Garrett
11. Jillian DuBois
12. Julie Nee
13. Jesi Stracham
14. Jessica Perez
15. Katie Scott
16. Kristin Smedley
17. Maggi Welham
18. Melahni Ake
19. NaTasha Pepper
20. Nicole Ruiz
21. Rachel Baribeau
22. Sharon Hughes
23. Tami Matheny
24. Tamesha Allen
25. Tory Holloway
26. Vallye Adams

MY SUPERHERO
Chip Baker

"You can do it, yes you can!"
-Wanda Baker

A superhero is someone that carries themselves in a superhuman way. They may look like a normal person in their day-to-day actions, but when it is time to put on the cape or change in the booth, they are ready to make an impact on the world. A superhero knows that life is bigger than them and that they are capable of saving the world. A superhero can come disguised as an everyday person, but underneath their clothes, they have an S on their chest. They have magical powers that are incomprehensible, and when turned on, they blow you away with what they can do.

Being raised by a superhero in my house was a blessing. My mother was my hero and exhibited some dynamic traits that have influenced many. I would like to share some of these traits with you.

Carry Yourself Well

"Don't ever mistreat anyone because you don't know who you will need to help you one day."
Wanda Baker

My mother was my superhero, and she carried herself well. Her ora was as if she was always floating on air. She would move about in a magical way. It seemed that everything she touched turned into gold. When she was out and about in the community, kids, parents, or people would see her and just smile. I would hear kids or adults using bad language. Once they noticed my mother in their presence, they would apologize to her because they respected her so much. She always had a smile and a positive attitude regardless of any hardships she was going through; this showed me that it is important to carry yourself the right way, regardless.

Work hard

"Hard work pays off."
Chip Baker

My mother always showed us by her actions that anything was possible if we worked hard for it. I can remember as a young kid how she would hustle to make ends meet. She would have three to four jobs at the same time: just pure grind and hard work. My mother was an educator, volunteered for different groups in the church and the community, minister of music at our church, worked at a corner store, helped students complete college paperwork, helped adults complete various financial paperwork, developed a GED program for adults in our town, and was the first black lady on the city council in our hometown. She always used her talents to benefit others.

I can recall one story of her working hard. It was early on a Saturday morning. We all had a long week in school and various church functions. My mother woke us up while it was still dark outside. She said, "Get up and get dressed. We need to go get the church van." I had no clue why we were waking up so early, but like so many other times, I figured it was to help. As my sister and I hurried and rushed to the car, we proceeded to put our belongings in the seats. We rode over to the church to get the church van, and then we proceeded to Blackshear Elementary School. The school was the pride of our community because it used to be the "Black" high school back in the day. As we were there, several adults from all age ranges arrived in the parking lot. They then came over to pile up in the van. As they were getting in, my mother greeted them with a smile and phrases of encouragement. Some were, "Good morning, let's go do this," or "Glad you made it, are you ready to go knock it out?" As I observed this, I still had no idea of what was going on. After a few minutes of people loading up in the church van, we began to go for a ride. Along the ride, I heard one guy say to my mother, "I am nervous, but thank you for helping me and believing in me, Mrs. Baker." Another young lady said, "My mama is going to be so proud of me when I pass this test." I was still trying to figure out why we had to rise from a deep sleep so early; a sleep after a long, exhausting week. I was very cozy in my comfortable bed at home. Oh, and did I say that it was still dark when we woke up to get the church van? Lol!

I started to observe and piece some of it together. These are adult people that my mother is taking somewhere to take some type of test . . . hmmm. We continued to drive for about forty-five minutes, and, finally, we got to our destination. When we made it there, my mom parked the van, got out, and walked the adults into this small school. She got them all signed in, and then we hung out in the school lobby for a few more minutes. A couple of the adults were watching my little sister and me; one young man said to me, "Your mom is a good lady!" Again, I had no clue what he meant and why he said that. As everyone was beginning to enter the classroom, where they would take "the test," my mother said to them, "Good luck, God Bless you . . . You will do well!" She then looked around and said, "I will be outside in the van waiting for you."

So, of course, I had lots of questions while we were in the van waiting. The main question was, "What kind of test are they taking?" She explained that the people she brought here came to take their General Educational Development (GED) test. For some reason or various circumstances, they did not finish high school or get their high school diploma. The GED tested their high school level skills and was an alternative to getting a high school diploma. Blown away and highly concerned, I asked my mom, "So you have been working with them to help study for this test?" She said, "Yes." I was like, "So this will help them get better jobs?" She was like, "Yes, and will help them take care of their families."

As they started to come out, they all had smiles and positive body language. They all seemed grateful for the opportunity to change their lives forever because of the hard work my mother had put in for them. In reflection, this was one of the first signs that showed me that this lady really was a superhero with superpowers; superpowers because of the hard work she put in to benefit others.

Live and Learn

"Life is all about living and learning."

Chip Baker

Superheroes live and learn. Not only did my mother help others get their proper education, but she also continued to get higher levels of education herself. She worked on and received her master's degree from Prairie View A&M University while I was in upper elementary and junior high school. She completed her degree when I was in the seventh grade. She would take us to her Saturday and night classes. I was responsible for watching my younger sister, who is four years younger than me. We got the privilege of getting to watch the amazing Prairie View band practice and often perform while my mother was in class. It was a blessing and privilege to explore campuses of some of the top educational institutions because she took us along with her. The experience made a huge impression on me and showed me that it was always important to live and learn. I was enamored by the climate and by what I saw on those campuses. Everyone was always nicely dressed and extremely cordial. I would see professors carrying briefcases and students with nice new shoes. You could tell who the athletes were because some of them would have on sweatsuits, tee shirts, and shoes that matched. They took pride in representing their university.

I also remember staying in a motel for a few weeks of the final semester of her master's degree. It was the first summer session, and my mother had to be in the classes every day so that she could complete the program. We stayed in the motel during the week and then took the two-hour drive home for the weekend. My mother had to be back to do choir rehearsal and then play for the church services on Sunday. This routine went on for several weeks.

It was hard for a lady, but even harder for a black lady to get opportunities in those days. But she stayed persistent and got an opportunity at a Regional Education Service Center in East Texas. There she trained teachers and provided resources for the school districts in that region. She then received her principal's certification from Texas A&M University. She was always pushing herself to make things better for her family. Living and learning were important to this superhero.

Crazy Faith

"Faith gives me humility. Self Confidence gives me the ability to execute. Faith and self-confidence are key!"

Inky Johnson

Superheroes have crazy faith. My mother wholeheartedly, with everything she had, believed in God and had crazy faith. There were times when we did not have all we needed financially, but she still went above and beyond to give to others. She would organize holiday food drives for the church and community while we did not have much at our house to eat. When she got her mind and heart set on something, there was nothing that could stop her from reaching the goal. Sometimes, when we would need things that I knew we did not have money to take care of, my mother would say, "Pray about it, baby . . . God will provide." There were times that I needed money for certain things, and I had no clue how it would get taken care of or managed. Examples of those were SAT and college recruiting trips. Somehow, she always had faith, and things worked out. In my mind, I knew that my mom could not afford to pay for me to go to school. If I did not receive any scholarship money for school, I would go to the military. She would say, "Don't worry, son . . . God will provide." My mother would have crazy faith that it would work out. Along with her crazy faith, she put in the work to do extra jobs to ensure that everything worked out for her children. My superhero had crazy faith!

Have Great Relationships

"Life moves at the speed of our relationships."

Pastor Danny Green

Superheroes have great relationships. My mother knew that her mission was bigger than she was, and she treated people in that manner. She had amazing relationships and gave everything she had to people and received the same effort in return. As her kids, my sister and I have received lots of benefits from her treating people the right way. People loved my mother so much that they also loved and cared for us. She took care of the kids in our school and community. She also took care of the adults and was always open and willing to help others. Because she was so great, we received some neat experiences and benefits from that.

Eventually, I got an opportunity to be Head Coach/Athletic Director in my hometown. There were so many people that supported me. I am sure it was because of what my mother had invested in them or their family members. I recall one experience that completely explains the ripple effect of that. One day I was in my office and received a phone call from this man. He told me his name, but honestly, I don't recall who he was. He said, "Your mom was my teacher, and I loved that lady. She was great to me. When I was a kid, I used to go fishing and bring her fresh fish." He then said, "Give me your cell number, and when I go fishing again, I will bring you some fish." I didn't think much of it. I was appreciative of the call and knew that my mom had made a positive impact on many. About three weeks passed, and I got a call on my cell phone from this number that I did not recognize. I answered and said, "Hello?" The man on the other end of the call said, "Hey Coach, this is the guy that your mom taught that called you a few weeks ago." He went on to say, "Man, I caught a bunch of fresh fish, and I have some for you. Bring your son out to my house, and I will cut and clean them."

So went to his house a little outside of town, in the country. We pulled up, and he was accurate; he did have LOTS of fresh fish. He walked us over to this huge cooler and said, "Pick out the ones you want." So, my son and I picked out some nice jumbo catfish. He then took my son over to his cleaning and cutting set up and began to show my son how to do the whole process of cleaning and fileting the fish. That was one amazing experience that we will remember forever. I tell you this story because my mother chose to invest in that relationship and be great to him. Subsequently, my family was able to experience the benefits of her great relationship. We now have a great relationship with that guy and his family. That is why it is important to have great relationships and treat people the right way, regardless. My superhero had great relationships.

"There is a cause and effect for every action. Choose your actions wisely."

Chip Baker

Cause and effect are inevitable in our lives. Because we influence people, it will make an everlasting impact on their lives. It will last for generations to come. Because my mother was a superhero, she influenced me. The effect was that her influence deeply affected me and put me on the path to be the person that I am today. My hope is that I make her proud daily by carrying myself the right way, working hard, living and learning, having crazy faith, and having great relationships.

Just like she influenced me, I also hope you can take the lessons she taught me and apply them to your life. They will allow YOU to be a SUPERHERO for the people you influence and impact.

God Bless you on your journey! Go get it!

Traits of a Superhero

Carry yourself well.

Work hard.

Live and learn.

Have crazy faith.

Have great relationships.

ABOUT THE AUTHOR:

See Lead Author's Bio in About the Author section.

A MASTERCLASS OF INSPIRATION WITH INSTRUCTOR DR. JAMES LOLLAR

Aisha Foy

"For decades, retiring Professor James Lollar has helped students realize their potential." My heart dropped as I read this headline posted from Dr. Gary Shirr's LinkedIn account as I was scrolling on social media one day. It was an article from Radford.edu announcing the retirement of a Radford University Marketing Professor that changed my life forever. I was impressed at how "on point" the description was of his career, describing it as helping students realize their potential. However, to say that he helped me recognize my potential was only the beginning.

On March 10, 2021, I sent Dr. Lollar a text to get his mailing address so that I could send him a copy of my first book that was inspired by the impact he had on my college experience. I was thrilled to inform him that my desire to grow as a person and help others do the same came from his class, and I was excited for him to see the finished product of what was first inspired by him. A few months later, he texted me to inform me that Fall 2021 would be his last semester at Radford. Immediately, I began reflecting on the moment I walked into his Professional Selling Class, in the fall semester of college, at the age of nineteen. I was coming off a life-changing summer of being a Quest Assistant, which is the name of a Freshman Orientation Leader at Radford, and I was hungry to continue my journey to self-discovery and self-actualization. Boy was I led to the right class.

7,511 is the number of students that Dr. Lollar impacted throughout his three decades of being a marketing professor. However, his approach to teaching business made me feel like the curriculum was designed just for me. My experience in his class can single-handedly be the top reason for any success that I have as an individual; let me tell you why. I walked in his class hungry, ambitious, and driven; however, one of the biggest flaws that hindered my growth was the ability to connect with others and effectively communicate with people who were different from me.

I was starting an internship in the ticket sales office in our athletic department, so I was eager to learn a few sales tactics to help me in the role; this was the class that contributed to a huge part of my personal development. I learned that great salespeople are intentional about serving others. This class brought to my attention that everything in life involves selling. I remember vividly one of the first lessons of professional sales is personal growth. I also remember the emphasis of learning that if you want to be good at sales, you must be good at identifying the needs of others.

Dr. Lollar wanted to ensure that sales were less about you and more about serving others. Thus, my journey of not only helping others succeed began but becoming obsessed with mastering the skill set needed to be able to understand what was needed from me began. It is one thing to want to help others, but it is another thing to have the ability to actually help them.

If you follow me on Twitter, @GrowWithAisha, you may sometimes see me randomly tweet out, "Listening is a skill," after probably some irritating understanding that not many people truly know how to listen intently. Listening is one of the skillsets that I take pride in having, and I continue to navigate the professional world. I understand how much of a blessing it is to have Dr. Lollar emphasize the importance of it. Although sometimes I want to take credit for it, I know for certain that listening would not be a strength of mine if it weren't for him.

His class also introduced me to the two authors that saved my thinking and changed my life forever. We were given reading assignments and projects that had nothing to do with making money. One of the first assignments Dr. Lollar had us do in class was a book project. The first book is titled, "How to Win Friends and Influence People" by Dale Carnegie. This book alone was the catalyst for helping me interact with people and build relationships at a high level. I have always been a misunderstood and extremely direct communicator. Often, I would end up in arguments in which I would decide to engage in an important conversation with someone who saw things differently than I did. In the experience of reading and writing a reflection paper on this book as a class assignment, it became transparent that I was doing wrong in my human interactions. Not only did it improve my relationships, but it also saved them.

That experience sparked a fascination with self-help books and personal growth, which inspired me to choose another book to dive into from the list that he provided. The second book that I decided to explore on my own was the legendary "7 Habits of Highly Effective People" by Stephen Covey. I cannot properly explain the difference this book made in my life. The biggest lesson that I took from it was to "seek first to understand, then to be understood," which is a principle that I hold on to daily to help guide how I try to impact others.

Every day, Dr. Lollar's class was a masterclass of inspiration; however, there is one more project that stuck out to me as a lifesaving, mind-shifting experience. As part of an assignment, we had the option to visit a gravesite. The reason for that, I believe, was to understand that life is short, and it will become a time where we aren't here anymore, and we have to ask ourselves, what legacy do we want to leave? What do you want people to say about you when you are gone? What impact do you want to have? This exercise was also to help me develop a sense of urgency to live each day on purpose and not waste any time going through the motions. On each grave, there is a dash in between the date that you were born and the date of your last day on earth. So, we had to ask ourselves, what do we want to do with that dash? The class not only showed me that sales were service, and professional development was personal development, but it shifted my mind to a place that it has never been. It saved my past relationships, enhanced my current ones, and gave me the tools to develop ones I wouldn't even have the capacity or awareness to develop.

I am currently pursuing a career in college athletics with dreams of becoming a Head Women's Basketball Coach; however, Dr. Lollar inspired me so much that I almost wanted to become a college professor so that I can impact students in half of the way that he did. In my first book, *Success is My Major, Start Entitled, Leave Unforgettable*, I pose a personal growth professor inspiring my students to be students of personal growth before being students of their profession. That pursuit alone will lead you to a professional career beyond your wildest imagination.

Eight years later, from the time I met him, still reflecting on the impact that Dr. Lollar had on my educational experience, it was interesting, but not surprising, that his approach was very intentional. And that before I even stepped foot in his classroom, he was on a mission of his own.

Dr. Lollar grew up in Samantha, Alabama, and was one of twelve children. He was a first-generation college student and earned his bachelor's degree, master's, and Ph.D. in marketing. Dr. Lollar began his career as a graduate teaching assistant at the University of Alabama, then served five years as an assistant professor at the University of Georgia, and then twenty-nine years as a professor of marketing at Radford University. Throughout that

15

time, he kept a roster of each of his students, which shows his commitment and dedication to his craft.

His career as a professor is the true definition of a legacy. Here I am, a young professional living the life of my dreams aligned with who I am, dedicated to personal development because of the intentions of someone else. I realized that my experience wasn't exclusive after reading so many testimonies of other former students of his, living similar lives, and maximizing their potential. The fact that you can feel someone's intentions as if they were meant for you is a total demonstration of someone living their purpose. This inspires me even more.

If the chapter in this book does anything for you as the reader, I wish to encourage student-athletes or all college students to embrace the whole college experience. As a Division 1 student-athlete, it is very easy to get so caught up in being a college athlete that you forget to be a college student—understanding that because of your athletic ability, you now have access to amazing Professors. I was not a business major at Radford University, but boy, did the business professors there change my life. I must say that I am certainly lucky that I did not allow basketball to get in the way of building awesome relationships with people like Dr. Lollar, who has had more impact on me than any athletic endeavor will ever come close to, at the end of the day. Other professors at Radford University include Dr. Danylle Kunkel, Dr. Gary Shirr, Dr. Kevin Ayers, and administrators like Joel Hanlon, Laura Turk, Ellen Taylor, and last but not least, Former President, Penelope Kyle. You all, amongst others, played a huge role in my educational experience at Radford University, 2012-2016.

Finally, I want to encourage you as the reader, to embrace the journey of becoming unforgettable, and if we want to reach our full potential, then we have to embrace and accept that the results of our life's work are not to benefit us, or this journey is going to lead to a never-ending cycle of confusion and entitlement. We, as leaders, must let go of the idea that our mission is to benefit us and understand that we may never reap the benefits of our intentions. Once we have accepted this, we can fully live a life dedicated to *impact*.

ABOUT THE AUTHOR:

Social Media:
IG @ growwithaisha_
FB @aisha.foy
Email aishafoy@gmail.com

Aisha Foy is recognized for her leadership skills and for motivating people to achieve their goals, as well as for her basketball playing career. As a student-athlete, Aisha was determined to prepare herself for what was next. While basketball was her first true love, the light bulb that went off in her head sparked an obsession for leadership and personal development.

These discoveries came as a result of the adversities that Aisha faced being out on her own and her growing pains. She turned her failure into success, and with those lessons learned, she was driven to motivate others. Aisha has discovered the secret to getting ahead is getting started, and she wants to share those insights with the next generation of students.

As a student-athlete, Aisha received honors like:
- Nominated NCAA Woman of the Year 2016
- First Team All-Big South
- Radford's Athletics Senior Leader Award
- Selected Who's Who Among Students in American Colleges and Universities
- Won the Center for Diversity & Inclusion Established Leader Award.
- Received Division 1 Full Basketball Scholarship
- Completed four internships in college as a Student-Athlete
- Founder and President of Independent Women Achieving Goals in Education

Aisha has an undergraduate degree in Sports Administration and a master's degree in Higher Education. No matter her job title, Aisha wants to help teach lessons to young people and motivate teams to be their very best. Aisha's perspective and servant leadership nature stem from her mother, who is a community leader in Norfolk, VA. She is the Founder and Director of an AAU Girls Basketball League and has grown the organization to be nationally recognized for developing college and professional girls' basketball players.

Currently:
- Author: Success is My Major
- Success Major Motivation Podcast Host and Owner of Personal Growth Membership SuccessMajorMotivation.com
- Black Excellence in Sports Podcast Co-Host

THE GOLDEN TRIO
Alecia Thomas

The love of family is unconditional and long-lasting. It allows one the opportunity to grow and learn from each other while molding and strengthening an individual. As a child, family is what I reflected on to model my character. Children learn from their parents and family, and they mirror the representation of who they see as their parents. Children also crave support, motivation, encouragement, desire, compassion, influence, and love. These characteristics allow them to feel a sense of who they are, or sometimes, who they don't want to be, which promotes or hinders their growth and development. Most importantly, family is a part of you. Friends also become family by building life-long relationships.

In my childhood, I admired and closely observed three women in my life. I refer to them as The Golden Trio. The word "Golden" reflects their royal beauty and character. Together, they were women of faith, love, and respect—a "Trio." They were always encouraging others with their gems and wealth of wisdom. All three women were givers of themselves and willingly helped others. As a kid, each of these women was family to me, but they each had their own purpose.

The Golden Trio represents Wanda Walton (Mama), my mother, Doris Johnston (Meme), my maternal grandmother, and

Lois Aimes (Grandmother), my paternal grandmother. They are the epitome of God-fearing women.

Mama would say, "If anybody asks you who I am, tell them I am a child of the KING! My passion is using genuine concern and love to minister to God's people! Thereby, inviting HIS Spirit to abide!" Her genuineness and love of God taught me the compassion and loving energy I have for God and his people. She was a fearless woman full of faith and determination. Her boldness, as a kid, showed me that she could pray and ask God for anything and "he'd always show up and show out," as she would say. Mama was full of grace, patience, and love.

Meme was a determined, strong-willed woman. She'd often say, "Baby, when you know better, you do better!" Her determination spoke volumes. When I was in her presence, I felt that I could achieve anything. Her articulation of words illuminated a feeling of joy and excitement in my spirit. She'd always assure me that I was the best. In all things, she would always remind me how much she loved and appreciated me. Her expression of love and appreciation was beyond measure.

My Grandmother was a woman of small stature, but mighty in love and gratitude. In my youth, I remember that visiting Grandmother's house was a joyous occasion. She'd always have gifts for her grandchildren. To me, it didn't matter what the gift was; it was the fact that my granny thought enough of me to bless me whenever I was in her presence. As a kid, I felt loved, welcomed, and had a sense of belonging. I knew every visit with Grandmother meant I was taking home something special that she had just for me. Her gift of giving reminds me to bless others by taking the focus off myself and putting it on others.

"I've learned that people will forget what you said, people will forget what you did, but people will never forget how you made them feel." – Maya Angelou

Women of Purpose

The Golden Trio instilled family values in me, which helped me identify and form meaningful and trusting relationships in my life.

Through their dedication to God, prayer, love, and guidance, many lessons were learned such as: be humble in all things, do things wholeheartedly, and you'll be blessed; always approach obstacles positively, and you'll be greatly rewarded; be kind and genuine to everyone because you never know who and how God allows others to be in your lives; speak life and be cautious of your thoughts and words; help others that are in need; be thankful and grateful, and never complain about anything; be passionate about what you're doing; always do things with a purpose; give to others, and allow your service, spirit, and words to bless others.

The Golden Trio allowed me to witness the importance of family prayer, togetherness, interactions, connections, and trusting one another, which created unbreakable bonds and defined the culture of my family. Family teaches you how to be grateful and thankful. Being in the presence of The Golden Trio blessed me with an abundance of wisdom, passion, understanding, and growth.

Our legacy starts with who we are as an individual. Today, I am continuously reminded of the women Mama and Meme were by people whom they were able to bless with their presence. Be it through their harmonious sounds of music, their knowledge of wisdom, or their faith, they've left an impact on the communities they served. God allows us to be the light for others in times of their need.

Being raised in a Christian home gave me an understanding of how to live, serve God, and have unyielding faith. These women helped me become the woman of God I am today. I am a woman of faith who trusts God and faces adversity with hope. I know of his interest in my life. I am a woman of faith who is confident because

I understand the divine plan of my Heavenly Father and my role to bless lives. I am grateful for all things.

Mother

You've always been there to love and model the way.

You've led me well, spread your poise, and created for me such a loving and caring space.

It will never matter how far we are apart; we will always share matters of the same heart.

You'll never be forgotten; that simply can't be. As long as I am living, you're always with me.

Your light always shines safely in my heart.

I know that you are shouting and walking with me along the path I tread.

I am who I am because of you.

ABOUT THE AUTHOR:

Social Media:
Email ootieb@yahoo.com

Alecia Thomas is a fourth-generation educator. She has served students, families, and teachers in education for years and currently serves as an Assistant Principal.

She grew up witnessing the educational and positive impacts her mother, grandmothers, and great-grandmother had on people and their academic success.

They influenced her to become a dedicated, compassionate leader. Alecia believes that education is the key to success in life, and teachers make a lasting impact in the lives of their students.

She married her college sweetheart, Paul Thomas Sr., and has four children: Ronnie, Paul, Braylen, and Auriana.

FIVE HEROES FIVE LESSONS
Amy Anderson

"The strength of our success is built on the strength of our relationships."

Gene Burton

The tapestry of my life is woven with the relationships found therein. Looking back on my journey, I can see now how essential relationships were at every turn. In addition to the amazing traditional family, I grew up in, there are people who were integral in the development of who I am. I am changed by the lessons they taught me. I learned these lessons from their wisdom and example. My leadership is greatly impacted and fueled by their stories crossing into mine.

When I reflect on my core values as a leader, five relationships shaped me. I am forever grateful to them for their lasting footprint on my life.

Encouragement

I was very fortunate to be close with my grandfather. One of the lessons I learned from my grandfather was a principle I consider essential when working with people. The lesson came to me after my grandfather passed away. He passed unexpectedly, and we were grief-stricken. We held a vigil at my grandparents' home until we felt that my grandmother would be able to stay by herself again.

One of my grandfather's friends came by whom we had not met before. He came in and entered the den where we all sat. He said, "Which one of you is the basketball player?" My siblings pointed to me. He looked at me and said, "he told me all about you, every game that he ever came to see you play. He was so proud."

I know that his friend moved from person to person in our family home that day, but I only heard the story about me. Make no mistake—there was no question about how my grandfather felt about me and all the ways he loved me. But hearing his love from someone else's lips was an incredible gift. These words created the next level of encouragement for me. I learned that day about the power of the spoken word of encouragement, not just to the person who is being complimented, but to someone else entirely. I learned that there are many ways to show people you love them and to encourage them. I have to think this experience changed the way my grandfather's friend viewed our family. The example that was set made a positive impact on every side. It was a way that love kept showing up in my life.

My relationship with my grandfather continued to be an influence on my desire to lead with love. My memory of how he felt about me, coupled with the words he spoke to me and about me taught me the power of speaking life into people. In my leadership, I tried to find ways to speak life to someone who might be overlooked, in a slump, or even the underdog. I found that speaking this belief into people would not only raise their confidence but their performance.

As a leader, I truly believe that your decision to speak life into others is a decision that's about you, and never about them. Speak the good to those who deserve it and to those who don't. Make the decision as a leader to lead while planting seeds of hope.

Composure

"Keep it on the hardwoods, Wilson." Most of my high school memories live in my mind as things that happened between basketball practices. I lived for those days, and my time in athletics was vital in developing my leadership abilities.

At our high school, the locker room was downstairs, below the gym floor. Practices during the season started at 6:30 a.m. We arrived in the dark, clumsily dropped off our gear in the locker room, and made our way up two flights of stairs to the floor of the gym. I remember my heart rate picking up as I started to climb each morning, wondering what waited for me and if I was ready, and I was excited to get after it.

Many a leadership lesson has been written about experiences on a field, a court, or a locker room. Mine comes from a coach that changed my life, sheerly with her expectations of me and what she believed she could will me to do. Donna Capps was her name, and tough love was her game.

After some practice, I felt invincible. There were plenty of other days when I left wondering why I was even in high school, much less a member of the basketball team. There were days with player spats and turnovers, and goodness we all know there were days we hit the line because of our mistakes. Whether it was one person's mistake or the entire team, we would hit the line.

On those bad days, each of us had a choice when we left that floor. We could do what psychologists call "stinkin' thinkin'" and let those mistakes dictate the next few hours. Or we could set our mistakes aside and focus on a new day ahead of us. We could use our mistakes as an opportunity to either turn towards our teammates or turn against them. Out of all the lessons you learn going through that type of adversity, each day, a lesson from Coach Capps stuck with me.

She pulled me aside one day and said, "Keep it on the hardwoods, Wilson." Confusion was evident on my face, and I was probably fifteen years old at the time. She said, "When you head down those stairs, leave it here. The mistakes you make on the court don't define your life, and neither do the victories, for that matter. Leave the disagreements and struggles that you have with your teammates on the gymnasium floor. When you walk down those stairs, walk down together, unified. Disagreements are ways that we learn and grow together. Leave it on the hardwood."

This concept shaped my thinking, and it still does to this day. Serving on the superintendents' cabinet is no easy task. Behind the closed doors of a cabinet meeting, team members often battle every side of the issues at hand. To solve problems on an executive team, you have to bring every perspective to the table, including perspectives that are different from your own. This practice is essential to the success of the organization. In the best of situations, team members leave the conflict "on the hardwoods." They walk out unified, committed to a relationship and unity for the good of the students.

Many times, I thought about my coach saying, "Leave it there and move forward with your day." The ability to do this strengthened me as a leader. This philosophy strengthened my relationships with my colleagues. My desire to create this atmosphere for the teams I served helped new opinions and perspectives to come forth. As leaders, if we are worried about offending others and making sure we don't disagree, harm will come both to the leader and to the organization we serve.

Successful organizations have healthy disagreements, and they move forward together. Speak the unspoken, ask the question and come to an agreement together. When you leave that table or that room, leave the hard discussion behind. Leave as respected colleagues and be thankful for the opportunity to work with people who care less about their egos and more about the good of the whole.

I don't know if Coach Capps knows that she taught me that, but she did.

Vulnerability

The popcorn president—that's how we knew him. He was always giving away popcorn, using popcorn as a vehicle to welcome us to our university, connect with us, and remind us that we were in a family. Dr. Newbury was a people magnet. He was charisma in a bottle, and he was the President of the college I attended.

Dr. Newbury was the first leader I remember really noticing and watching with amazement at who he was. As I look back, he was one of the first people, which made me think, "I'd like to do that." Dr. Newbury changed the culture of the little college I attended one person at a time. He created excitement and a feeling of success by showing up and being present in our lives.

One of the best gifts that Dr. Newbury showed us was his use of self-deprecation to draw people to him. One of my favorite memories was hearing Dr. Newbury speak. He would throw out his first joke trying to warm up the crowd. If laughter was scarce, he would look up, pause, pull a pen out of his lapel, and mark the failed bit out of his script, while still at the podium. As the speech went on, the laughter of the crowd increased with each strike out on the page, and he won us over. He knew the power of putting your misgivings on display, and he put those who poked holes in his role as president out of a job.

He lived vulnerably. Even the act of passing out popcorn could have been a failed bit, but he did it with his heart. He wore his heart not only on his sleeve but out on the sidewalk in front of his house. His mission was for every student to know that we had a family in the place we chose to go to school. We knew we were loved by an imperfect person who had our best interests at heart.

Dr. Newbury was never participating in a planned public relations event; it was just who he was. Dr. Newbury taught me to let my life be a billboard of vulnerability. Be vulnerable, laugh at yourself, and draw people in. It's worth it, and the stories last forever.

Coaching

Before executive coaching was chic and listening was a coveted skill, there was Deborah Smothermon. She fielded calls from school administrators day and night, night and day. They often needed a hand, a moment of calm, or a sense of clarity. Although there were situations that needed a wise response like, "If I was in your shoes . . ." she mostly just listened.

She was my supervisor. There was no doubt that she was the one person I never wanted to disappoint. All the same, she showed me how powerful listening can be for a leader. Having a person committed to listening to you was powerful because a school administrator's circle is very small. The proverbial circle of trust actually gets smaller as you move up the chain.

In truth, in my experience with helping leaders grow, what they need the most is their own voice. Not your voice, and not mine but theirs. They need it more than any system or leadership guidance in the entire world. Dr. Smothermon taught me that allowing leaders to hear their voice is a gift that you have to be strong enough to give; you have to hold back on your advice and mantras. Your experiences play second fiddle to the questions they need to ask to bring out the heart of the situation.

I've heard too many times that supervisors cannot be coaches. People say it's "too messy, too time-consuming, too soft." I couldn't disagree more. I am a product of someone who didn't think so either, and I have never had expectations so high as when I had the honor to work for her and her leadership team. Coaching is a foundational practice for me. If you want to feed a man for a day, give him a fish. If you want to feed him for the rest of his life, ask him to tell you what kind of fishing he does best.

Courage

Sometimes, you come across someone who can leave a legacy in the lives of those they serve. That's the way it was with Dr. Burton. He was the most beloved superintendent our little town has ever known.

Ironically, he was the one who did the hardest work behind the scenes, and when faced with hard decisions, he dared to lead from the front. When the situation called for it, he asked us what we thought, and he listened. When the decisions were clear, it was his voice and his heart that took the heat. He would never put us in a situation that he had not been in first. He had such a high level of personal accountability for himself you couldn't help but do the same.

The changes required for a small town to become a big town are difficult and emotional. Every day, you see failed redistricting attempts, petitions, and board meetings on the news, all resisting change. Many leaders decide to keep themselves far away from the battle, fearing that it may impact their ability to lead. This type of self-preservation actually takes more away from their effectiveness as a leader than standing up and sharing their vision.

There's an old saying that reads, "Mistakes are mine, victories are yours." Dr. Burton truly lived that. He tried to deflect victories and give them to the people he served. We all knew the vision that he had for us. He poured his heart into us, and our success was his success. He had the courage to believe in those he served when we couldn't believe in ourselves. If we failed, he dared to fail with us, pick us back up and send us forward to try again. When we did try again, he stood behind us until we got our feet back under us. I could only hope to live this type of legacy for a few people. much less for the thousands of people that he impacted. It's never about you; it's about the people and the students that you serve. Their success truly is yours. As Andy Stanley says, "If your leadership is all about you, it will never live beyond you." Dr. Burton was a "beyond you" leader, and I am better for it.

I'm still building my legacy, and it will continue to be made up of the relationships that cross my path. I am so fortunate to reflect on these lessons and share their impact, just as my grandfather taught me.

"Your giftedness and grit determine your potential. Your character will determine your legacy."

ABOUT THE AUTHOR:

Social Media:

IG @amysdreams48

Email amyruthand@gmail.com

Amy Anderson has more than twenty-five years of experience in education. She served as a chief on the Superintendent's cabinet for seven years in a 6A school district in the DFW area. She has served as a principal for more than ten years and in a multitude of roles in education.

Amy wants to follow her passion to help educators become transformational leaders and reach their potential in whatever role they serve. She wants to help people find their own voice and confidence in the unique abilities they bring to their work. She regularly designs learning for groups around executive leadership coaching, school culture, and goal attainment. Amy offers innovative learning institutes for leaders in various stages of their careers. Her passion is coaching and mentoring teachers, coaches, school principals, and executive leaders.

Amy currently works for N2 learning, focusing on supporting leaders who want to transform their organization through executive coaching and individualized professional development. In addition, Amy teaches at the University of Texas at Arlington in their Educational Leadership and Policy Studies program, where she designs relevant learning for future school administrators.

Amy is a frequent speaker at a multitude of conferences, including the Texas Association of Secondary School Principals, the Texas Council of Women School Executives, the Texas Association of School Administrators, and the Texas High School Coaches Association. Amy is a wife and mother to three children.

TRANSFORMATION TAKES TWO
Amy P. Kelly

The first thing I heard on the phone was a long, exasperated sigh.

I was calling to get input from someone who worked for my potential boss. When I introduced myself and shared the purpose of the call, their response was not what anyone would interpret as a positive start.

As I inquired about this person's experience working for my potential employer, the entire conversation had a negative tone. My next call to another past employee was a mirror image of the frustration and contempt from the first call.

It did not seem like the people who worked in the position I was considering enjoyed their experience working for this individual. Even though both people said positive things about the company, they made nothing but negative comments about the boss.

Nonetheless, something inside me was demanding I press onward.

The position and the company were interesting, and there was much about the industry I wanted to learn. During the interview process, I listened to my potential boss and got excited about the opportunity to help him address the organizational priorities tasked to his team. I could sense he knew his stuff, and his dedication to the executive team and the organizational mission was evident.

That intrigued me. Why did those in this role in the past have such terrible experiences? What could I do to help this company and this interesting and committed person I saw in front of me? Could I do the job and make an impact? Was I ignoring valid red flags? Why did everyone say he was such a jerk?

What I heard from past employees contradicted my impression of the interview. Even with the conflicting inputs that would normally be a cause for concern, something continued to nudge me forward.

After taking the risk and accepting an offer for the position, it was my opportunity and responsibility to produce results. Over time, I experienced a transformational shift in the way I viewed the manager-employee relationship. This shift became a pivotal lesson in my career. It is a lesson that shaped my leadership skills, and it is a lesson I use every day to support others in their career development and overall success.

The first step in this shift was moving from inward thinking to outward thinking. I stopped believing that the only one with influence was the boss. I stopped thinking about my challenges and started considering how to create solutions for my manager's challenges. I started seeing challenges as opportunities to contribute.

It was a shift toward a more mature role in the workplace combined with a commitment to support someone who appeared to have a couple of his own growth opportunities (as we all do). I also had to believe that I had the power inside me to be a catalyst that could help others, even people with more experience and knowledge. I needed confidence and humility. I needed to take my mind off myself and focus even more on helping my boss. I needed to not be afraid to make a mistake or look stupid as I learned.

Eventually, I trusted my own impression of my boss over the criticisms I heard about him. Focusing on the good, I did everything in my power to learn what he knew about the industry. I strived to help others on our team and to pinpoint the objectives and measurements of success for my position, our team, and the organization. This was not easy because, of everyone in the company, I knew the least about the industry.

I listened and kept my comments to a minimum. I started to see it as my responsibility to see the best in my boss no matter what, and this may not seem like a huge shift, but it is the opposite of how many people view the manager-employee relationship. And, if you think I am saying this to seem heroic, I am not. I am just sharing the opportunity we have to shift our perspective to supporting the boss instead of the boss being there to support us. Still, he did not make it easy with his tough and direct approach. For many, many months, I received no positive feedback from him.

My manager knew his role, understood the company, and genuinely wanted the best results for all. He also had exacting standards, limited patience, and no problem holding others accountable. Sometimes, his direct communication style included statements that came across as unnecessarily harsh and were close to being HR-noncompliant. Despite his toughness, if you listened, took action, and did not take his style personally, it was easy to see a big heart beneath his razor-sharp approach.

For months I observed and took in everything I could. He handed me old reports to read and shared electronic files with short email messages like, "Somebody tried this before," or, "You might want to read this." He also asked me, "Did you meet with this person?" and, "You could make a substantial difference if you helped this person or this team." He guided me and pointed me in the right direction, but he never gave me a blueprint. He trusted me and empowered me. He said things like, "Make a plan, and show me in our next meeting." He also told me to start over many times.

He never sugar-coated anything. I was never sure what to expect when I went into his office, but I made sure I was as prepared as possible. It was not uncommon for him to say, "Why would you do that?" or "Wrong, try again," or, "Do not do that. Don't be a knucklehead." Over time, I noticed that he did not magnify my mistakes. He asked me a couple of questions and gave me the opportunity to readdress the issue.

I witnessed him speaking to others with impatience and unfiltered observations. He also did this with me. I made sure not to react or take it personally. I did not babble on with justifications and explanations. I was concise with my updates because he did not want a long story. He wanted to know what I did, what the results were, and if I needed anything to get the objectives accomplished. He had a lot to teach, and I was committed to him, my team, and the objectives.

When I made mistakes, he asked me questions to get me back on track and defended me to others in the company without trying to ignore my mistakes. He just had my back and allowed me to get it done right. It only made me want to do more to deserve his loyalty and confidence. I observed his style to improve my work.

Our part of the organization was responsible for operations, technology, human resources, and learning and development. People would come asking for promotions, new titles, and raises regularly. It was educational to listen to the questions he asked when people came to present their thoughts and make their demands. I started to understand that he did not care for people asking for raises and promotions. It was his opinion that if you got results, you could trust the leadership team to pay fairly and look for ways to advance your career along with the company's growth.

I tried to use what I learned to help people inside the company find the best avenues for promotion, increased compensation, learning opportunities, and new challenges. Being a part of a high-performing team is an unforgettable experience, and sometimes people overlook the value in that aspect of their career. I worked to share that perspective with others related to being a part of the team in a high-growth company.

I used the lessons learned to help others reach their career goals and push them toward a position with an even higher level of career success. My manager's rapid-fire questioning style helped me create business cases that were better positioned to support the promotions, raises, and other types of advancement opportunities people were looking to get. In the process, everyone had challenging and beneficial business conversations.

Along the way, there were times when people in the company would speak badly about my manager or would try to magnify something negative that happened based on a decision or action he took. I decided never to participate in those conversations. When I was present, I would either leave or present an alternative view on how the courageous and creative business decisions he made might be something others had not fully explored. I would encourage my coworkers to be grateful that our boss was willing to experiment with his decisions and to expand the potential of our company. He was always doing what he thought was best for the organization and the people.

This may sound weird, but I learned to love this boss, the other people in the company, and the entire experience. It made me think of how people in the military who share experiences where they gain so much respect for their team that they consider it a type of love. My human resources career has taught me not to have conversations about love in the workplace, but what I learned is that trust and personal accountability are types of love you can give at work. It is a way to put your dedication and commitment into action. These are the highest investment you can make in your career.

You must have trust and personal accountability to be a great manager. You must have trust and personal accountability to be a great employee. You must stay committed over time to learn and grow to best performance together. This experience was the first time I saw this combination in mutual action, and it was all wrapped up in the decision to believe the best of my boss and to act accordingly. All along, I thought I was helping my boss. All along, I worked to stop thinking about goals, promotions, or compensation. All along, I wanted to use what I learned to help others achieve their career goals.

As the years passed, I started to see the transformation inside of me. It was because of both of us—my boss and me. We both committed to believing in each other and stayed the course. We backed it up with action, loyalty, and a sincere desire to see each other succeed along with the organization and everyone in it.

The transformation was beyond what I ever imagined, and it has been influencing my career ever since. It was amazing to see both of us grow and change. Someone who I had been told was a horrible boss turned out to be the best boss I ever had.

It all started because of a person with exceptional business skills and a lot to teach someone that would listen, act, and demonstrate ability and loyalty. The belief this manager had in me made me believe in myself and my ability to be helpful, support others, and make a valuable contribution to a business. I took the belief he had in me, cherished it, respected it, and did everything I could to make a difference for the business and the people in it. I wanted him to be right, and his belief is what made it possible. Then, I desired to share this type of belief to help other people and businesses grow.

He made a difference in my career when I thought I was making one in his; however, to maximize the influence of our transformation, we both needed to be committed. The impact of that influence is still felt today.

One of the greatest workplace joys is seeing someone being appreciated for their contribution. Watching a peer grow their career, expand their salary to take care of their loved ones, and fulfill their life's purpose is an extraordinary experience.

As a part of this book, filled with the impact of influence, here are some of the lessons I learned from this leader who was known to be the worst and turned out to be the best. You can use these tips to grow and to help others do the same.

Here are three key takeaways about using your influence to create a positive impact in the workplace for a more positive world:

1. Be loyal. Make it about your boss. There are a ton of people that bash their boss and blame them when things do not go their way. Many times, people demand promotions and blame their boss if it does not happen in the way they want. Instead, give your manager loyalty, consistency, and attentiveness. Few people acknowledge how hard it is to be a manager. Employees don't often empathize with their bosses but instead react with judgment and ultimatums. Try to imagine how hard it might be in your manager's shoes. If you want to grow, believe in your boss. Make it about serving them. Growth and development exist in committing to help those above you succeed.

2. Be patient. Do not grow weary if the things you want do not materialize in the timeframe you would like. Keep doing great work and believing that your boss notices. Keep believing that the reward is what you do to make it easier for your boss and the people on your team. Be consistent in your outward focus. In time, your patience will yield all kinds of results.

3. Build up your boss and bring solutions to the table. Do not get distracted by the noise. Look beyond the communication style of your boss as much as possible. Be willing to focus on the goals and move forward. Rather than complaining about your boss's shortcomings, create a plan to make a difference.

The impact of your influence will cause your boss, your team, and your organization to grow and get stronger. And you will too.

ABOUT THE AUTHOR:

Social Media:

IG @amypkelly1
FB @amypkellynews
Email amypkelly@amypkelly.com

Amy believes in people and supports them in becoming the leaders they were created to be. The "P" in her name stands for the middle name she received from her grandmother Pauline and symbolizes the power inside of each person to fulfill their purpose. Amy is the Vice President of Consulting for The Jon Gordon Companies. She is a co-author of _The Energy Bus Field Guide_, which is a roadmap to fueling your life, work, and team with positive energy. Her second book, _G.L.U.E. A Leadership Development Strategy to Bond and Unite_, is a short story about faith, personal growth, and forgiveness. Amy's work is focused on growth and optimal performance for individuals, teams, and organizations. She was recently published in the Association for Talent Development's Global TD Magazine, _Mindset Shifts for Better Human Performance Improvement_.

Amy is a global human resources and talent development executive known for building exceptional talent and cultures, including award-winning employment brands and leadership development programs. As Vice President of Human Resources, she led the HR and talent development function as part of executive teams completing the successful sale of two enterprise technology distribution companies.

Amy is a graduate of the Leadership Coaching for Organizational Well-Being Program at George Mason University's Center for the Advancement of Well-Being. She brings over twenty years of experience in human resources, learning and development, business development, and coaching to develop industry-leading executives and the cultures to achieve their objectives. Amy designs and implements leadership programs and is a certified GPHR and SPHR through HRCI where she shared her C.R.E.A.T.E. process for how HR leaders can build leadership development cultures. Amy is the co-creator of the Leading Well leadership program, a holistic, systems-thinking approach to the practice of effective leadership and personal wellness.

Amy is an active member of the Society for Human Resource Management and completed the SHRM Foundation Veterans at Work Certificate Program.

She is a global facilitator for the Association for Talent Development ATD in the areas of Improving Human Performance, Change Management, Human Performance Improvement, and Training.

Amy is a Gallup Strengths Trained Coach and certified in leadership and EQ programs.

You can work with Amy as a leadership development coach, career coach, speaker, facilitator, and Human Resources/talent development/culture/change management consultant. She speaks on topics including:

- Leadership and Team Development
- Positive Culture
- Teamwork
- Mindset and Performance
- Change Leadership and Resilience

You can find Amy believing in people and partnering to build high-performing leaders and organizations in all aspects of life, whether at home with her husband and four children, in her community, or in businesses all over the world. It is her passion to believe in people and work alongside them to drive performance at the highest levels possible.

STACCATO
Andrea Bitner

I read once that "change is inevitable; growth is optional." When I was twenty-one years old, I innocently believed that I was fully grown. Yes, sir, my checklist for life was complete! I got married, completed my college education, purchased my first home, landed my first teaching job, enrolled in a master's program, and created a plan to start a family. I was ready to tell anyone who would listen how to be successful, *just like me.*

For the first quarter of my life, I had only known people, places, and things who were just like me—Italian, middle-class, studious, conscientious, righteous, ambitious, religious, and positively infectious. The tiny bubble that I floated in from experience to experience was harmonious. I never skipped a beat. Inside of my bubble, life was glorious!

As I launched into the world as an educator, wife, mother, and friend, I quickly learned that my enthusiasm for life had created a series of bubbles. Yet it seemed that, no matter what I tried, I couldn't keep them from popping. *No one out there was just like me.* By the time I was thirty-one years old, my life plans hadn't just popped—they had exploded.

Somewhere between my righteous perspective and relentless pursuit of happiness, a crisp, loud, inflamed staccato halted my predictable daily harmony. I signed divorce papers and put my house up for sale. I searched for a new full-time job to support us. I grieved over the loss of time with our two little ladies as they learned how to split their time between two loving parents. I crawled out of bed in the morning and shed tears of guilt and sorrow at night to encourage sleep.

I had absolutely no idea what I was going to do or how to do it. I had lived my life on the same dance floor for thirty-one years. All of a sudden, I felt several emotions at once—envy, caution, fury, anxiety, confusion, and ignorance. Every rock I could find called my name because all I wanted to do was plow down as deep as I could under it.

Meeting Art saved my life. After a chance introduction at a university campus event, we quickly became best friends. He was unlike any human I had ever encountered. He walked here from two thousand miles away. He was a world traveler, a hard worker, bilingual, somewhat educated, poor, and happy. He truly believed that "life was beautiful," and he strived to see the opportunity for beauty in every person, place, and thing that he experienced. Anytime adversity showed up, he would smile and respond, "Ahhhh. Life is beautiful." This statement baffled me beyond measure. He was my polar opposite. Without a concrete plan and a blanket of security, life could not be beautiful!

Through Art's stories of diversity, adversity, and adventure, he challenged me to stretch a muscle that I had never built—how to accept, adapt, embrace, and grow through life's changes. Spending time with him motivated and terrified me. How could he happily live life on his own without a plan, a checklist, resources, or a safety net? Why wasn't he running as fast as he could from any sign of a risk?

As years passed and our friendship continued, he gently encouraged me to step onto new dance floors and grow my spirit. I slowly began to lean into his example. At first, I dipped my trembling toes into a new arena; I learned how to be a single mom and live alone. Then, I began to waltz. And I bought my own house. I quick-stepped into a new teaching position. Soon I traveled to different countries and spent time with happy people who had much less than me.

In time, life began to feel like a samba! I listened to new music and read more books. I learned how it felt to try and speak a different language. It felt wonderful to open my eyes and ears to the larger worlds dancing right next to us. I realized what I loved most about others was that no one would ever be just like me. I became a stronger mother and independent thinker. I wrote a book and had it published! No longer did my journey need to occur in synchronous harmony. I learned that staccatos are necessary and fun!

Now, at age forty-one, I can say this: thank you for your impact, Art. Thank you for teaching me that when we fail to adapt, we fail to move forward.

Now I am curious, spontaneous, courageous, joyous, and found. Without you, I would have never realized that it is the embraced growth during a change that allows life to become beautiful.

ABOUT THE AUTHOR:

Social Media:
IG @andreabitnerbooks
FB @andreabitnerbooks
Email 4andreabitner@gmail.com

Andrea Bitner is a proud wife and mother of two beautiful daughters. She lives on the East Coast among some of the fastest-speaking people in the country! Her first book titled, "Take Me Home," was released in July 2021. This book tells the true story of eleven of her former English Language Learner students. They give a firsthand account of what it is truly like to become bilingual in America!

She has worked with students in grades K-12 from all around the world through her twenty years in public education. Her work as an English Language Teacher, Reading Specialist, Literacy Coach, Presenter, and High School English Teacher inspired her to continue to share the great news: Learning a second language is an asset, not a handicap! She hopes to inform, influence, and inspire all readers and leaders to continue to be a champion for all stakeholders in the education community around the world.

DEVASTATED TO DETERMINED
Deidre Vasquez

I am blessed to have had many great influencers in my life. Parents, teachers, coaches, you name it, have all been part of shaping the person I am today. I am beyond grateful for them and truly appreciate what they have done for me, but there is one event I can reflect on that has been the dominant driving force in my life.

I grew up through my pre-teen years in rural southeast Ohio. We lived in a cul-de-sac at the bottom of Mac Drive in a modest house with three bedrooms. The neighbors all had kids my age, so my brother and I spent many days outside playing from sunup to sunset. I remember mostly playing kickball in the cul-de-sac (boys vs. girls) and loving the aspect of competition. In fourth grade, a couple of my friends encouraged me to sign up at the local elementary for the basketball league. I really hadn't played a lot of basketball but had played in a baseball league, so I thought, what the heck, let's give this a try. I ended up liking the sport. Before long, I asked for my own hoop and ball; thankfully, my parents obliged. I began to follow the Boston Celtics and The Ohio State Buckeyes and could not wait for their games to be on television. Basketball was becoming an intense passion. It was exciting for me to watch and play.

I continued to realize my love for sports the next few years. I loved to run (even though I wasn't fast), ride my bike, and play games in the cul-de-sac with my friends. My parents were in a church volleyball league, so I even became interested in that sport. Competition and sports were fun for me.

Fast forward to seventh grade, when I could join the team for my school and play against other schools. It was far more formal than my previous experiences. I tried out for volleyball and made the team. I remember putting on the uniform for the first time and feeling so excited and nervous all at the same time. As the season progressed, I really enjoyed staying after school for practice and playing in the games. November rolled around and junior high volleyball season ended. A week later, I had basketball tryouts. I remember being nervous, but confident. I felt like I had played a lot of basketball and was prepared to make the team. Try-outs lasted two days, and the team roster was posted the next morning. I woke up that morning with great anticipation. I hustled to the bus only to sit through a forty-five-minute ride to school. Once I finally arrived at school, I quickly went to the walkway between the gym and the main part of the school to confirm my name was on the list. I looked and looked for my name, but it wasn't there. I remember rubbing my eyes and again looking at the list. At this point, my heart was racing, and I was in disbelief. It was hard to breathe. I remember thinking, 'where's my name, where's my name.'

It was devastating to walk around school an entire day with my heart broken and wanting to   cry my eyes out. Finally, as I sat in Mr. Harper's history class, I heard the buses pull up to take us home. I held myself together until the moment my foot stepped down off the bus at the top of Mac Drive. I ran ahead of my friends and tears started flowing. My mom greeted me at the door, and I ran to her arms crying uncontrollably.

Not making the team was a hard pill to swallow, but every day when I got home from school, I practiced basketball. I was outside with the floodlights on at night, packing snow onto my basketball to make it heavier, and shooting it into the hoop. I ran track for the school team that year with the goal to get stronger for basketball. I was determined to make the team at the eighth-grade tryout.

After much hard work, determination, and mindset changes, I tried out and made the eighth- grade team. From that point on, I knew that there would be no one that could stop me from achieving my goals. No one would ever be able to take my passion from me or steal my joy. I learned, if I was willing to put in the work, that I could make anything happen. In high school, I went on to play on the junior varsity (JV) team as a freshman. I played varsity my last three years of high school. I was even fortunate enough to earn a scholarship to play at Sam Houston State, a small d-1 university in Texas, for four years.

Little did I know, that day back in November of 1985, when my heart was completely broken, was a blessing for the rest of my personal, athletic and professional life. You see, I am a high school basketball coach and have been one for over twenty years. I relive November of 1985 every year during tryouts. I despise the day that I have to tell a student that she did not make the team. I do, however, have a face-to-face talk with her and encourage that student to work on her game and come back next year to try out. Sometimes, I share my story and let her know that anything is possible with hard work and determination.

ABOUT THE AUTHOR:

Social Media:

FB @deidrevasquez

Email dvasquez@conroeisd.net

Deidre Vasquez is a successful high school basketball coach and math teacher. She enjoys working with teenagers and helping them realize they are capable of accomplishing anything they put their minds to and can achieve all of their goals.

FAITH OVER FEAR
Denise Franco

My hero growing up was so cool and so smart. He could do no wrong in my eyes. Unlike other kids' favorite heroes, mine didn't wear a cape, and he wasn't in comic books. My hero was my big brother.

Unfortunately, one day he decided to start experimenting with recreational drugs, and things got bad quickly! When our parents tried to help him by sending him to therapy or rehabilitation facilities, he would rebel and come back worse. I slowly became a very angry child that would lash out against the adults in my life.

I lost faith in God at a very young age. Due to my brother's drug addiction and deteriorating mental health, I lived a large portion of my childhood in a very chaotic household. There was constant shared energy of fear, confusion, and anger. When he needed more drugs, he would steal from us to pay for his vices. Imagine coming home after school to find your VCR player, mom's car, and your piggy bank all missing, knowing exactly who took it and why. That was my life growing up for many years.

There was a constant fear in our household for his life and the lives of those around him. Every time he left the house, there was an eerie energy that filled our home. On one hand, there was a sense of peace because he wasn't there to fight with us and create chaos. On the other hand, there was a deep feeling of fear that he wouldn't make it back alive, or worse, that he'd hurt someone while he was out being reckless.

One time, he came home black and blue from head to toe. He said that he had been "jumped" by a gang of guys until he was knocked unconscious. Then, they left him in an empty lot, in the middle of the desert. They left him there to die. By the grace of God, he eventually came to. In his frail state, he had no alternative but to climb the six-foot gate and walk at least a mile before finding his way to a friend's house. Luckily, someone was there to answer the door, and they made sure my brother got home safely.

At times, he would also try to get better and do better. It never ended well though. The withdrawals were brutal. The depression would kick in and his suicidal thoughts would take over. My parents had to hide everything that could be potential harm to him or others. This included over-the-counter and prescription medications, kitchen utensils, knives, and even pencils and pens—things you would never think of as dangerous. Every once in a while, he'd get hold of something and lock himself in the restroom for hours. It was the scariest when a bottle of pills went missing. Sheer fear and panic filled our home on those days. All the while, my little sister and I were there, absorbing every emotion, sensing every fear, and witnessing every suicide attempt. My parents were so busy trying to keep their son alive, my sister and I felt forgotten a lot of the time. But can you blame them? Nevertheless, we were angry and hurt, and we were left to deal with our own traumas as best we could with limited support and resources.

Thankfully, that same trauma has kept me away from experimenting with drugs, for the most part (except for marijuana, but that's a different story for a different time). This was probably for the best since I found myself falling into seasons of depression. One day in my early adulthood, I was struggling with one of my most severe bouts of depression to date. I felt like I had nobody. I felt like I had nothing left to give. I didn't think I deserved to live, nor did I want to spend one more day on Earth. I wanted to end it.

There was one little problem—I was pregnant at the time, and I didn't want to hurt the baby. So, I reached. I reached as far as I could reach, and I prayed to a God that I did not believe in to help me get through this low point in my life. I prayed that he would take all my ill thoughts away and that he would help me birth a healthy child.

He did. I didn't kill myself, and I gave birth to a healthy baby girl, Alyna. After I gave birth to my first and only child, a lot of things changed for me. One of the greatest shifts I noticed was my motivation to be better and do better so I would always be able to provide for my little family.

A few years later, I decided to dive into the self-development space. One of the first pieces of advice I received was, "Find Someone That Has What You Want, and Do What They Do." At the time, I was about twenty-five years old, a single mother to my then four-year-old Daughter. I had just quit my full-time job so that I could focus on figuring out how to become successful in the Real Estate industry, and I was Broke, BROKE.

So, I started researching "Rich and Successful Women." Naturally, I came across Ms. Oprah Winfrey. Oprah Winfrey was named the first Black Woman Billionaire in the world in the year 2003 by Forbes. That was the first time that had ever been accomplished! She was later named the world's ONLY black billionaire from 2004-2006.

Ladies and gentlemen, I grew up in America. I have witnessed up close and personal how hard it can be for a black female to make a name for herself and get ahead in this country. So yes, I was highly impressed. I wanted to break barriers that were even a tiny bit as impressive as her achievements. I figured if I could learn anything from her and get even a small crumb of her level of success and financial stability, I would be happy.

I quickly began to realize that it wasn't the millions of dollars that she earned that was most impressive about her life. It was the person she had to become to achieve all these accomplishments. It was about her journey. Did you know that Oprah was sexually molested as a child? Can you imagine living with a trauma that intense growing up? The thought alone makes me feel physically ill, and I have a tremendous amount of solace for her.

I understand what it is like to live in a constant state of fear in your own home, but the fear she faced was far different than what I experienced. When I learned this information, I found I had an even greater level of respect for her because of her ability to move past her traumatic history. She instantly inspired me, and I wanted to be like her. And if I'm being completely honest, I also felt like her hard times trumped mine. So, "If she could do it, I can do it," became my new motto. Just like that, the daydreams about becoming an amazing woman as Oprah began.

I wanted every piece of advice Oprah's ever given! I started looking up any and everything that she's ever put her hands on. Her books and interviews were my go-to sources, and they did not disappoint. I went as far back as I could find. When I heard something that resonated with me, something that touched a soft spot in my gut, I listened. I stopped what I was doing and re-played the clip or re-read the section. I tried to understand the message to the BEST of my ability, and then, I digested the fact that this was an area of my life that needed work and I quickly got to it.

Oprah's messages in so many words told me to grow spiritually. They told me to go and look for MY TRUTH. Not the truth that the world projected onto me, but MY INNER MOST TRUTH. Grow Spiritually? Grow Spiritually.

I knew this was going to be a challenge. You see, from around the age of twelve to about nineteen, I claimed Atheism. I claimed it loud and proud for many of those years. If you asked me then, there was no heaven and there was no hell. There was no God and no Devil, and if you asked me then, I would tell you that there is a scientific reason for everything and that people believed in God for the same reasons they once believed in Santa. He was a "feel-good fictional character." "But what about the Bible?" people would ask. "It's there to guide us not to do things that are immoral in life, like don't lie, don't steal, don't cheat. It's a moral compass for a bunch of common-sense stuff." I had an answer for EVERYTHING, and you couldn't tell me anything! Nevertheless, I accepted the challenge.

I had to have an open mind about the process, and it took some time. I have since then re-connected with "the source", as Oprah likes to call it, and I've truly come to enjoy learning and growing Spiritually. Through her teachings and advice, I learned the fundamentals 1.) Do Everything with Intention 2.) There's Something You Can Learn from EVERYONE 3.) ALWAYS Practice Gratitude.

I've also been pointed in the direction of Gary Zukav, Gabrielle Bernstein, Mel Robbins, Maya Angelou, Jay Shetty, Tony Robbins, Michael Todd, and many other brilliant minds of the 21st Century. Gabby Bernstein taught me to release my expectations of the outcome. She taught me that the universe has something greater in store for me. Tony Robbins and Mel Robbins constantly remind me to get rid of the excuses I create for myself. Maya Angelou reminds me not to shy away from my innate feminine beauty. Jay Shetty reminds me to just breathe. Michael Todd inspires me to have crazy faith, and Gary Zukav has affirmed that life truly is magical. I'm sure these people have a few things in common, but if there's one thing I know for sure, it is that these people lead with love and faith.

My journey in self-development has been an ongoing process since the day I decided to dive in. It has helped me elevate to higher heights than I could've ever accomplished through the teachings of self-development alone. In large part, I have Oprah to thank for motivating me to take that leap of faith. Her story is so inspiring that she was able to get through to me after so many years and so many other failed attempts. I really appreciate her for that.

Since then, I have become more aware of the responsibility that comes with being a successful leader. I am more aware of my impact on those around me, especially my loved ones. I understand now that my level of success is not measured in dollars and cents, but in the energy that I can create and hold in my space, what I do with that energy, and how I share it with the world.

I try my best to do EVERYTHING with intention every day. For example, I'm more than just a "Realtor." I am a Real Estate Advisor and a Trusted Consultant. Whether my clients choose to put their trust in me because of my resume, what I stand for, or after being referred to me by someone they know and trust, I am trusted with decisions worth hundreds of thousands of dollars daily, and I don't take that lightly. It can be an intense and stressful job at times, but sharpening my craft truly is a labor of love for me and I walk in faith every step of the way.

My spiritual journey has also helped me better understand the torture of resentment and the art of forgiveness. Forgiveness is beautiful and underrated in our modern-day world. In my pursuit of forgiveness, I have been able to forgive my brother for both the decisions he made in his past and the ones he still makes today while trying to find his way through this trip we call life. I've forgiven him for the pain he inflicted on our parents, the horrible things he said and did in his altered state of mind, and the time I felt he "wasted." He has been just as influential in my life as Oprah and all the other spiritual teachers I referenced before. I'm so grateful for all the lessons he's taught me, the unforgettable memories we share, and for his ability to pull through the hard times, even when it felt easier just to end it.

I've forgiven my parents for their perceived faults and shortcomings as well. I realize now that being my parent is only a small part of their life journey, and they've done their best to figure it out. I appreciate the effort that they have put forth and continue to put forth for all their loved ones, despite all the hard times and heartache.

The most liberating person to forgive was me. I've forgiven myself for all my "less than perfect" moments, the things I said when I was angry and didn't know how to express myself, the mistakes I've made in the past, and the people I've hurt along the way. I have learned that forgiveness is for oneself. It is one way that I can show myself love instead of allowing myself to drown in an ocean of sorrow, guilt, and anguish. Being a human with a story worth telling requires us to make mistakes. But like Oprah says, "Failure is just God's way of gently letting us know that we're moving in the wrong direction." So, listen to the guide, but be gentle. Forgive yourself for your shortcomings. If you intend to live a life of adventure, there are sure to be more up ahead.

To Oprah: Your teachings have been a great foundation for me to build upon. Your words of wisdom have given me "permission" to seek out MY Truth and feel empowered in the process. I now understand that we ALL have contagious energy, and I want mine to be as radiant and empowering as yours. Thank you for speaking your truth. Thank you for your vulnerability and humility. Thank you.

To You, The Reader: SEEK YOUR TRUTH. Silence the noise and do the inner work. I wish you all the success, joy, and peace in the world, and I hope that you, too, decide to lead in love & faith.

With Lots of Love,
Your Friend, Denise.

ABOUT THE AUTHOR:

Social Media:

IG @ddenise_ffranco
FB @denise.franco.965
Email franco.a128@gmail.com

Denise has been home frown in El Paso, TX, and the surrounding areas for most of her life. She was born into a low-income, predominantly Hispanic family. She was initially introduced to Real Estate as a child. She watched her father and uncles work on the construction, rehabilitation, and maintenance of both residential and commercial properties. She also had the opportunity to watch as both of her parents worked their way up into the middle-income tax bracket and become homeowners for the first time. Although they didn't take the traditional home-buying route, she made a very clear observation that with her parents' newfound home ownership, there was a different pride of ownership. There was more privacy and space and an overall better family dynamic after the move. This planted a seed for Denise.

Denise has been active in the real estate community for over seven years now. She has had the opportunity to learn all about the different opportunities that real estate has provided not only her clients but her peers, partners, and the El Paso community. She has since created a strong brand with herself organized team within the umbrella of one of today's most innovative real estate brokerages, eXp Realty. She has built a successful business by cultivating long-term, profitable relationships centered around referrals from past clients, partners, and her sphere of influence.

Denise and her team at The Franco Real Estate Group specialize in helping the El Paso community buy, sell and invest in real estate.

She and her team use their resources, tools, and expertise to walk their clients through each real estate transaction with honesty and transparency. They have also recently expanded their business to help serve the commercial and business owners of Texas and New Mexico with their investing needs.

Denise is also a Mentor in the eXp Mentorship program that helps newly licensed Realtors in her city get through their first three transactions with the oversight and guidance of an experienced Realtor. She especially enjoys sharing the unlimited opportunities that come with investing in yourself and Real Estate with other working mothers to empower and inspire continued growth.

SEE THE NEED, MEET THE NEED
Jeni Neatherlin

There is a reason you are reading this book. Know that whatever your reason is, there is a power and a purpose in it that has already been prayed over for you.

If you had asked me at age seven who the influencers are, I would have said the president, my teachers, Santa Claus, and Hulk Hogan (we watched a lot of wrestling). However, when I was a kid, you were important if you were in the encyclopedia. Oh yes, anything that was real and relevant was found in the A-Z glossy set of encyclopedias. An entire world of information, brought to you by the door-to-door salesman—power in print.

At fifteen, I would have said my influencers were my coach, famous people like Matthew McConaughey, and the cool kids at school (especially the ones with the coolest car or sound system). Any time I hear Salt-N-Pepa it takes me back.

In today's world, influencers use their cell phones and social media. Millions of people follow their every move. They look pretty, they entertain, and they were genius enough to make an entire profession out of doing that.

There are similarities and differences in those lists of influencers from the various stages of my life, but now I know that influence is really just nouns wrapped in verbs. It's people or things and what they do to shape our world. The reality is that you don't have to have a camera recording your every move, and you don't have to be in the library collection to influence. Influence is every day, every human thing.

It's not an exclusionary occupation or role; it's all-inclusive, and Jesus invites us all to take part in being a light for others. I hope that this book lights your wick so that you may stand close to someone else and watch them light up just because of you. That's my goal, each and every day. Light the wick. Burn bright.

Family members will always be your early influencers. I cannot write a chapter on influence without thanking and acknowledging all the gifts my family gave me. I have a giant family, and for that, I am eternally grateful.

My mom gave me a sense of high achievement. She was a survivor, and so much of my strength came from my mom. She stood up when she felt there was an injustice, and she helped me understand that no matter who the world says we are, our voice matters.

My dad made me a risk-taker and a dreamer. My sister gave me a fighting spirit and a good heart. My cousins gave me connections, roots, and friendships that would sustain me throughout my life. One of these cousins, who is a high school principal herself, is my best friend in the entire world.

My granny, grandma, aunts, uncles, nieces, nephews, and step-family have shown me what family means. Sometimes we lived in their spare rooms and on their couches. There were times when the presents under the Christmas tree and the clothes on my back were given to me by them.

However, my brother was the biggest influence on my life growing up. I saw him work as a teenager to pay for things for his little sisters. Big brother always paid. He gave the gift of his time as he coached me in softball. Not many nineteen-year-olds spend their spare time coaching their kid sister.

He paid for his own 1978 Ford truck but gave it to my mom when she didn't have a vehicle to drive while he was off at college.

He did that so she could take us to school and go to work. That left him without a car, so he had to ride the bus in a town that was hours away. My brother was my protector. He moved to San Antonio but spoke daily with our father, who lived in the same town.

I was at a graduation ceremony for one of my schools, and my brother asked, "Have you heard from Dad?" He was having a hard time reaching him. I told him I had not but would check on him when I was done working.

He called me a few minutes later and said, "Don't go, I have a bad feeling. I'm going to send our cousin." He made me promise that I would not go. I acquiesced.

Thirty minutes later, I got THE call. Dad was gone. Our cousin had found him. Not finding my dad like that protected my last memories of him. After he passed, the only thing we argued over while going through his stuff was his brand-new TV. It was nice, not gonna lie, and we both wanted it. However, the arguing was the insistence that the other take it.

"You keep it," I told him.

"No, you keep it," he insisted.

When I got home, I saw that the TV was already hooked up in my house.

My brother taught me resilience, stability, and the gift of sacrifice. He was the leader in our family. I learned that leaders look out for their people. Now, as a coach, athletic director, and head football coach, others benefit from his influence daily.

All of my family members gave me the ingredients to be successful. Their support and the environment that they created sustained me as I grew up. Well, I should say environments; we moved a lot, so we had many homes. I have moved almost fifty times in my life. For the record, that number does not match my age! I was a poor kid that constantly moved around and whose early life resembled the chaos of the novel, *Hillbilly Elegy* by J.D. Vance, then that of the Seavers from *Growing Pains*.

There's a lot in my life that I can't talk about in a chapter or a book. I was not able to unpack several experiences from my chaotic life until I was in my late thirties. Deep-rooted struggles can be a catalyst for change, or they can be a toxin that inhibits growth. You get to decide.

In the spirit of sharing, though, here goes: I grew up overweight, and I ate my emotions. I allowed growing up in poverty to shape my views on money. I had items repossessed, and my student loans defaulted. I stayed in relationships God did not intend for me to be in and ran from my faith. I fought with my sister, who I lost to a brain aneurysm at thirty. Yep. I've screwed up—a lot.

I have felt guilt, shame, loss, and fear. But, I am a survivor. I've endured failures, lack of self-worth, heartbreak, stupidity, the death of loved ones, selfishness, and more. God gave me grit and love! He gave me the ability to overcome. He washed away all of my sins and gave me a fighting spirit. I became a first-generation college graduate. I lost eighty-two pounds before I was thirty. Years later, I asked my brother why nobody told me to put the cookies down. He reminded me that nobody told me to pick them up, either—valid point.

I paid back my debts, fixed my credit, bought a home, and learned about finances; I became smart with my money, really smart. Now people ask me how to handle their money. I had to relearn everything I thought I knew about finances because poor people view money differently. It was a complete rewire.

I welcomed Jesus into my heart and allowed Him to heal the scars. I put my faith in Him. Through all my mistakes, I was humble enough to continuously learn from the people that God put in my life. There are a million quotes out there about the people you surround yourself with and how those individuals will influence you. Those quotes are not wrong. You are the company you keep, and poverty is like a vacuum. It will suck you back in every chance it gets.

While the family is one thing, we all have control of the friendships we keep; There is a quote by Brian Cain that I live by, "Control the Controllables." This is where I feel I am blessed beyond measure.

Early on, God put incredible women in my life who welcomed me into their homes for Bible study. From fourth grade to sixth grade, every Monday after school, I went to Bible study with friends. Girls I met in this period of my life have remained my friends and confidants to this day. Over the years, I have sought out friendships with like-minded people: achievers, the champions. However, I also seek out those that bring something to my life that I am missing. New vehicles have blind-spot monitoring, proven to save you from potential wrecks; my people do that for me.

Right now, we are hosting an exchange student from Belgium that has shown us how to be appreciative of the things that we so often take for granted in America. Her beautiful soul has been a wonderful addition to our family as she shares her world with us. Her presence has allowed my daughter and me to share our love and our home.

As an adult, I protect my environment and my circle of influence. A person's negative energy will rub off on you if you allow yourself to stay in that environment. And boy, am I lucky that as an adult, the person closest to me is my daughter. She is my biggest influence!

My daughter is a special human that recently accepted Jesus as her Lord and Savior and was baptized in the Llano River. She sees the world through the lens of Jesus. When we eat at restaurants that have run out of items, she feels excited for them and how much business they must have had.

Recently playing in a volleyball playoff game as a young girl, she missed her serve to help her team win the second set of her match. Then, in the exact same situation in the third game, she made her serves and led her team to victory. Winning was great, but her ability to move past her mistakes is the real triumph. That's my girl. Influence starts in your own home.

Education has been my calling since day one. I was playing school before I even went to school. School shaped my opportunities. I was always good at two things, school, and softball, so I made a career out of both. Teaching and coaching for ten years allowed me to truly understand campus culture and the needs of those doing the work.

Growing up poor helped me empathize and understand the needs of the kids. With my teams, we have successfully turned around campuses that have brought us accolades along the way. But the pride in that work isn't in the plaques on my wall. It's seen in the lives of the kids and the people I've worked for and with.

One of the biggest blessings for me was going to school with rich, motivated kids. I could hold my own with them, and being competitive, I strived to compete at their level. I learned in grade school that I could be called poor, but I could not be called stupid (brother excluded, you know how that goes); this is why I love public education. I was in classes with kids whose parents made more money than I could imagine.

One of my classmates was in Forbes as one of the newest billionaires. Talk about teachers teaching kids with very different needs. What world collides kids like me with kids who hung out with George and Laura Bush? These are kids who now run billion-dollar oil companies. My classmates in high school were all exceptionally gifted and intelligent people.

As a kid, I didn't want to be poor. I dreamed of a world where you didn't have to put groceries back because I didn't have the money; where I didn't have to worry about the electricity being cut off. I yearned to escape our generational cycle of poverty, and education was my way out.

As educators, we have to know that we can be the difference-maker for kids who worry about things beyond the walls of our school. Not all poor kids will be good at academics. They will probably dislike it because they may always feel behind and because school is structured while their outside world is not.

Covid shutdowns have exacerbated this situation. On my campuses, I reinforce this message: we will practice empathy without exception. We can't close all the gaps, but we can show them we will never stop trying. Poverty cannot be an excuse. Yes, there are many things about school that are hard for those in poverty.

It may be harder to get them over the threshold, but life is hard. They are strong—stronger than most.

Wherever I am, wherever I go, we find ways to see the needs and fulfill them. Do kids need a jacket? Get them a jacket. Does the child need a shower? Let them take a shower during class. But they have to do the same work as everyone else. Clothes are dirty? We can help wash them. Cranky from worries at home? As the teacher, I say, "Ok, I won't call on you today, but I'm going to tomorrow. Be ready."

These are simple and small practices that we try to lead with and show that we care about our students; see the need, meet the need. It's the basis of all human interaction. However, we will hold everyone to high expectations because the worst thing we can ever do to a poor student is to reinforce that their circumstances today will define their world tomorrow—a world they don't believe in or imagine. We must believe for them. We must love and empathize, just like Jesus does for us.

The influence of people or the influence of situations will create an impact upon us. We get to choose what we do with that influence. Being our best means living a surrendered life, allowing the light of ourselves and others to shine. As a woman of faith and a leader, I do not take the influence that I have been called to lightly.

I pray a blessing over you now and always.

ABOUT THE AUTHOR:

Social Media:

IG @jenineatherlin

FB @ JeniNeatherlin

Email nhawk72@gmail.com

Jeni Neatherlin is a believer, mom, sister, daughter, friend, and servant that resides in Central Texas. She is a lifelong educator that currently serves as the Superintendent of Granger ISD. During her career, Ms. Neatherlin has been recognized throughout the state and nationally as an exceptional educational leader.

Her accolades include the 2021 Texas High School Coaches Association Article of the Year, 2020 Highland Lakes, Locals Love Us Educator of the Year Recipient, 2019 H-E-B Excellence in Education Principal's Award State Semi-Finalist, a Former Life Changer of the Year Nominee, and an Honorary PTA Lifetime Member Award Recipient.

She speaks to leaders at all levels, including aspiring superintendents, administrators, and coaches, as she works with all educators on school systems that produce a positive school culture. She also advocates for building bridges between academics and extracurriculars. She owns a firm that assists districts in finding their athletic directors and head coaches. She prides herself on utilizing the team concept in all aspects of school life—Work Together, Win Together!

Topics She Speaks About:
- Master Schedules
- Student Support Systems
- Work Together, Win Together: bridging gaps for athletic and academic success
- Becoming a Head Coach
- Becoming a Leader

Consultant: Solid Oak Leadership

MOVE THE BALL
Jennifer A. Garrett

They say that two things in life are certain—death and taxes. But wait a minute, that's not all. There's one more thing that is a certainty, too: *life will not always go as planned.* That's a fact. Think about it. How many times have you set a plan in motion only for it to get derailed and not go how you envisioned? Ah yes, that's all a part of the twists and turns we experience on this curvy road called life.

When it came to my career, I always prided myself on being someone who had a plan. I set SMART goals, I knew what I wanted to be when I grew up, and I put together a roadmap for how I could achieve it. Little did I know that one phone call would completely change all of that and turn my world upside down. I'll get to that in a minute.

First, let me describe my original plan. For me, my big, long-term career goal was to be a Fortune 500 CEO. Pretty ambitious, right?

While it was a lofty goal, it wasn't something that was out of reach for me. In my twenties, I had opportunities to excel and climb the corporate ladder early in my career, landing a senior management job with a Fortune 50 company, The Boeing Company. My peers were in their forties and fifties, and yet there I was, excelling in a male-dominated field. I had been labeled as one of those "high potential employees" and earned a reputation for being a quick study and someone you could put in charge of challenging projects that could get the job done.

I learned early in my career that I needed to think of myself as the "quarterback" of the game, driving how I would advance instead of merely relying on others to promote me. I was always looking to differentiate myself from others, build up great bullet points for my resume, network with executives and senior executives, and link myself up with some accomplished mentors, including one who later became the CEO of Boeing.

Life seemed to be good. I continued to climb the ladder, and I kept crushing it on my performance reviews. I left the company for an amazing role within General Electric's Aviation division and continued to advance my career. The bullets on my resume got more and more impressive. I knew I was positioning myself on the path to one day achieving that CEO goal.

That's what I thought, at least. Now let's get back to that phone call that changed everything.

On the early evening of November 28, 2016, I was sitting in my dining room when my cell phone rang. I grabbed my iPhone and saw it was my mom calling. Instead of answering the phone, I said, "I'm too busy. I'll call her back later."

You see, I talked to my mom multiple times a week and didn't think there was anything unusual about why she was calling. But this time, it was different. Her purpose for the call was to let me know that my dad had passed away.

My dad was seventy-eight, had not been sick, and there had been no warning signs or indication that he was going to leave us soon; this was completely unexpected.

So, what happened? That morning, my dad told my mom that he was feeling great. Like many elderly folks, he experienced chronic pain and took pain meds. That medication made him drowsy, so he told my mom he was going to take a nap in the living room. An hour later, my mom was cooking in the kitchen, and my dad's cell phone rang. He didn't answer. My mom then checked his phone. She tried to wake my dad up, but it was too late. He had already passed. It was that quick. No warning, nothing. The lesson: *tomorrow is never promised to any of us.*

It always bothered me that I didn't answer my mom's phone call because I said I was too busy. While taking the call would not have changed the outcome, I still felt guilty for putting work first.

When my dad passed away, I did a lot of reflecting and realized two things. One, you are replaceable in the corporate world. Two, when you go, the world keeps moving whether you're in it or not. I had heard people talk about being replaceable before, but I never thought that applied to me, quite honestly. Was I naive? Yes.

Because I had been advancing in my career and had these stellar performance reviews, I thought, "Well, if I were to leave the company, it would be a huge gap. They would miss me." What I realized during my reflection was that while a company might miss me, the business wouldn't just stop because I was gone. They would find a replacement, and while that new person might not be as smart or talented, the company would figure it out and continue to operate in my absence.

I also realized that when my time was up on Earth, the world would also keep moving forward without me. That impressive resume I had been building wouldn't mean anything. I mean, who would care about any of these bullets I had on that piece of paper? No one else but me. The seven college degrees, the billion-dollar deals I used to work on, none of that would matter. When I was gone, no one would think about that resume anymore. What people would remember, though, was the legacy that I could leave behind.

So, what would that legacy be? Three years before my dad's passing, I had published a book called *Move the Ball: How the Game of American Football Can Help You Achieve Your Life Goals*. It was a self-help book discussing how football principles, strategies, and lessons could help people accomplish their goals in all facets of life, not just in business or their careers.

After that book was published, I had many opportunities to speak on my *Move the Ball* philosophies and methodologies in the corporate setting. But I really wanted to make an impact in the sports community. When *Move the Ball* was published, do you think anyone from professional or college football called me to know more about what I had to say or invite me to speak to their organization? Nope. Not one single phone call.

When I tried to reach out and network with people from the sports industry, none of them cared about what I could share with them as a woman who didn't grow up in a football family. Instead, people told me I was wasting my time. They said things like, "None of these players care about what you have to say," and, "If you were my daughter, I'd tell you to go focus on something else." I didn't hear people saying, "That's awesome, Jen, tell me more."

While these types of responses disappointed me, I wasn't devastated. I understood that not everyone was going to see my worth or align with my vision. This lesson holds true for all of us with anything in life. But here's the thing to keep in mind: *when someone doesn't believe in you, realize that their understanding or affirmation is not necessary for your progress.*

When people give you a negative response, you then have a choice to make—ignore their opinion and keep going or let them deter you from what you set out to do. I chose to do the former. I continued to publish content and show people how they could "move the ball" to pursue the life that they wanted.

I showed up every day being consistent with my messages and my actions. That's when the magic happened, and a transformation occurred. In the beginning, I thought *Move the Ball* was just going to be a book about football. Yes, I would book speaking gigs and hold corporate workshops to teach and train on my leadership methods, but that is as far as I thought it would go.

Over time, *Move the Ball* evolved from a book about football to becoming a movement about how the competitive athlete mentality could help you move forward in life. It was broader than just football. The *Move the Ball* movement represented hope and never giving up. It was about how your past didn't define you or where you could go in life. It was about taking ownership, showing up in every single moment like you were supposed to be there, and going after the life that you deserved.

In 2016, people started posting on social media or writing to me, sharing their accomplishments and how they had "moved the ball." They also started using the hashtag #movetheball in their posts, back when hashtags were a newer thing. It was then that I realized that *Move the Ball* had become a way of life for people. I knew this was the legacy that I was meant to leave behind. That Fortune 500 CEO job that I had spent over a decade working towards no longer mattered. It's funny how life changes things for you. I believe that sometimes our lives have to be completely shaken up and totally rearranged for us to reach the place where we are truly meant to be. I never thought that I would be doing anything but working in a corporate environment. I loved it, and I had been thriving in it.

When my dad passed away, that all changed, I realized my true purpose was influencing others through my *Move the Ball* movement. I told myself that one day I would quit my corporate job to focus on growing the movement and making a larger impact. After all, this was my legacy, so I was going to go all-in and leave my mark on the world.

Being a single parent with five kids, I couldn't do the super bold thing and quit my job right away. No, I wasn't going to set myself up for failure. I spent some time planning out the business aspects and started networking with super-successful entrepreneurs. While I was a lawyer, had an MBA, and had worked in multiple Fortune 50 companies, I had never run my own business and wanted to learn from those who had. Preparation is important in anything you do in life, right?

Making the leap from corporate was also a very difficult thing to do. While I was emotionally ready to go, from a practical standpoint, leaving my guaranteed income source wasn't easy. I had a good-paying job, and I was also the primary breadwinner for my family. So, you see how this could have complicated things. After pushing back my leave date a couple of times, I finally decided to do it. On November 5, 2019, which would have been my dad's 81st birthday, I hung up my corporate cleats and went all-in on growing the *Move the Ball* movement, never looking back.

I had a plan and was ready to execute it. But remember that third certainty I mentioned earlier? Life won't always go as planned, and that is what happened yet again. In March 2020, the world changed drastically and shut down because of the Coronavirus pandemic.

People asked me how my business was going and commented, "Wow, Jen, this is really bad timing for you."

My response was, "No, this isn't bad timing. This is just one more thing that I have to figure out, and I'm going to have a great story on the other side of it."

Remember what I said about choices? Well, I had a choice: let fear of the unknown and this pandemic stop me or keep moving forward. Of course, I chose the latter.

Every day I suited up with a positive mindset and was ready to take on the day. I approached every day with a focus on the things that I needed to continue to grow the movement and the brand. I didn't back down. I aggressively pushed forward. Determined to "move the ball," I knew I was going to be a leader who positively influenced others too.

I kicked off the *Move the Ball* podcast on February 3, 2020. The show released two episodes each week featuring conversations with professional athletes and successful entrepreneurs on how the competitive athlete mentality could help people to be successful in business, branding, and sports.

The *Move the Ball* movement continued to grow in popularity. Remember those people in sports who weren't interested in what I had to say way back when? That all changed.

Since focusing on the *Move the Ball* brand full-time, it's been crazy to see the number of professional athletes who have stood behind the movement and seen the value of what it stands for. Football players who have won multiple Super Bowls and college football national championships. The impact that this movement has made on the world has also been pretty incredible, and this is just the beginning. There is still so much work to do, but I know that I have stepped into my purpose. God has taken my greatest pain and turned it into my greatest calling.

Now here's the lesson for you: *tomorrow is promised to none of us*. Therefore, it is important that we figure out what our "why" in life is and that we live each day intentionally and in a manner that aligns with that vision. Once we have that clarity, it's all about taking decisive action.

People who walk with a purpose don't need to chase opportunities. Their light causes people and opportunities to pursue them. It's never too late to start something new, reinvent yourself, or change your destiny. Stop letting fear paralyze you and step into who you were meant to be. Get out there, live in your purpose, influence others, make your mark on the world, and every day make sure that you suit up, show up, and move the ball.

ABOUT THE AUTHOR:

Social Media:
IG @movetheball
FB @groups/wemovetheball
Email info@jenniferagarrett.com

Jennifer A. Garrett is an internationally recognized branding expert, host of the *Move the Ball* podcast, author of the book *Move the Ball*, and creator of the *Move the Ball* movement. She currently works with executives and professional athletes on creating powerful brands and using those brands to "move the ball" in business.

Prior to being an entrepreneur, Jen spent many years in Fortune 50 companies such as General Electric and The Boeing Company, working in executive-level roles in engineering, strategic planning, sales, marketing, and legal. Jen has seven college degrees and uses her education and corporate experience to work with global brands on strategic planning, M&A activity, and revenue growth.

Her degrees are as follows: B.S. in Electrical Engineering, B.S. in Biomedical Engineering, Master of Business Administration (MBA), Juris Doctor (JD), M.A. in Communication & Leadership, Master of Laws (LL.M.) in Business Transactions, and an LL.M. in Taxation. Jen is also currently serving as a lawyer (Judge Advocate) in the Army National Guard. Jen serves on the Board of Counselors for the University of Southern California (USC) Master of Business for Veterans (MBV) program.

Topics Jen Speaks On:
- Career Navigation & Development
- Personal Branding, Presentation Skills & Public Speaking
- Leadership
- Business Networking
- Stress Management
- Time Management

- Effective Business and Personal Communications and Writing
- Product Marketing
- Strategic Thinking & Growth
- Employee Engagement

Coaching Programs
- Business Coaching (Branding, Marketing, Strategic Growth)
- Executive Coaching / Leadership Development Coaching
- Public Speaking Coaching
- Interview Coaching (Job Interviews, Salary Negotiations, Career Navigation, Media Interviews)

THE ROADMAP OF JOY
Jillian DuBois

Driving a vehicle has never been an enjoyable activity for me. My parents were perplexed because I was not interested in getting my driver's license when I turned sixteen. As a matter of fact, I had failed my driving test twice. Obtaining that credential would have brought great responsibility for which I was not yet ready. Much to my surprise, I eventually passed a few years later and began my career behind the wheel at eighteen, no longer a professional passenger.

Don't get me wrong. I love being in a car. I enjoy road trips with my family. It is a controlled environment in which we can have meaningful conversations, catch up on the latest audiobooks, sing to our favorite tunes, and stop for snack breaks along the way. I usually am content as the co-pilot, willing to help navigate our journey together.

Before the digital age of the GPS, there were road maps. Remember those huge, paper configurations that, when unfolded, could possibly equal the length of an actual country? They never folded back neatly into place. There was always that struggle to find the correct direction of the creases. Maps were difficult to read, and disagreements erupted between users. The tiny print, small lines to follow, and the map legend created somewhat interesting obstacles to overcome.

Fast-forward to today. We are now a part of a generation that is dependent on a technological navigation system to tell us exactly where to turn, how long it will take to get there, traffic patterns to avoid, all done with a soothing voice of trust. Smart route planning requires nothing but a simple Bluetooth connection. No two-sided argument. Just reliance on that voice to steer us safely to the destination.

I have tremendous gratitude for the options. Just like using a paper road map or a digital GPS, we get the opportunity and freedom to choose which directions we will follow.

If only life were that easy. If only it were a matter of deciding which path to take and allowing every other detail to fall into place seamlessly. We could avoid the dead-end roads, construction zones, and arrive just as expected. Life would be fully intact.

The straightforward fact is that this rarely happens. The road we take in life is full of sharp turns, dangerous curves, and warning signs. The cautions are evident, but we don't always acknowledge them in time.

My road map of life has brought me to where I am today. Born and raised in the south, I was brought up as a church-going, Bible-believing, strong-willed young lady who lived and breathed family life. I had made plans to grow up and marry a man who loved me and to have a home filled with several mini-me children who called us mom and dad: nothing fancy, just an uncomplicated, joyful life.

My road map led me to a wonderful life partner who, after thirty years of marriage, still calls me the love of his life. Tim and I met in college through friends, and I sensed quickly that he was the one for me. I remember the first time we went on a single date together. He came around the car and opened the door for me. "Now, that's a man like my daddy," I thought. He checked all the boxes. He still does.

We were soon thrown some sharp turns. Our enthusiasm to fill our home with children turned to heavyhearted discouragement. My body was not physically able to become pregnant due to stage 4 endometriosis. Years of fertility treatments, visits to reproductive endocrinologists, and expectant procedures kept leading to a dead end. Those arduous years were difficult to navigate. It was lonely for both of us. I found myself overthinking the whys, how's, and when's of what would come next.

Each time I was 'late' for my monthly cycle, I would take a pregnancy test and spend those waiting moments anxiously planning exactly how I was going to tell my husband we were going to be parents. The emotional letdown each time continued to build until it became apparent that our dreams were wrecked. I could not share in the joy of friends' pregnancies and healthy births. I avoided meandering through the baby section at my favorite stores. I declined invitations to baby showers and shied away from Mother's Day services at church. It was too painful, and I created boundaries to protect my heart from breaking.

I don't remember the actual moment when we felt led to pursue adoption, but I recall it not as a desperate remedy, but rather as an open avenue to travel towards parenthood. We completed all the requirements. I created a portfolio that included a transparent biography and photos that displayed our home and culture. Our home went through an inspection process, we provided details of our lives that proved us to be fit for nurturing a child, and we were put into the database of an agency in the hope of matching with a birthmother.

We were prepared and poised to wait. Domestic infant adoptions could take several months, maybe even years. So, our spare bedroom was organized and arranged with minimal essentials for our soon-to-be child. The anticipation kept us feeling positive about our time of waiting. It was as if our whole life was on hold. But we were at peace.

Six months later, we received a call from our adoption counselor that we had been matched with a young lady who was seven months pregnant with a baby boy. She had reviewed our portfolio and decided to choose us. There were immense feelings of joy, paired with the fear of taking the next steps. We kept following the course before us with grace and faith.

Things were falling into place, and we became excited as the dream of becoming parents was soon to become a reality. Many surrounded us with prayers and encouragement, but some wanted us to be aware of the reality of possibly being brokenhearted if this fell through. We recognized that fact yet never let that deterrent become a roadblock in our path.

Our birth mother went into labor two weeks past the due date. A call came in that she was at the hospital and requested that we be present for his birth. Tim and I immediately jumped in the car and drove. We arrived shortly and found her in the maternity ward along with her parents. They had wanted us there. There was no doubt that we were chosen specifically with purpose.

Labor was intense for her. Over the next fourteen hours, her contractions intensified, but she was not progressing towards dilation. A Cesarean Section was mandated, and things started to move quickly. She asked me to come to the delivery room and hold her hand. I suited up along with her mother, and we were present for the surgery.

Words cannot describe witnessing the physical miracle of birth. It is astounding and simply amazing.

Our son, Austin, was born. Perfect and healthy. After we went to the nursery, the hospital staff permitted us in to watch them weigh and bathe him. It was incredibly humbling and surreal. A new life was beginning.

Our birth mother never wavered. Never changed her mind. Never lost sight of what was best for him. Before we were approved to take Austin home, we met together in her hospital room. We laid him down carefully and encircled him with our love as we prayed over his future and gave thanks for the gift of life.

Our family was now complete. We were full of joy and gratitude for this answer to our heart's deepest cry. It was as if our wandering had come to a peaceful, contented end. We had an immeasurable gift. One that we pledged our commitment to for the rest of his life. One of the conditions of our semi-open adoption was to send our birth mother a written update and photos each year. While we never heard from her again, I knew she had always received our messages of love. Each heartfelt letter concluded with the same sentiment:

> "And as always, our hearts keep you in our prayers and thoughts as we watch this young man, Austin, grow into a man after God's heart. He is sensitive, caring, loving, kind, gentle, and so much more. This gift you allowed us to raise as our son has been more than we ever expected or could ask for in life. I know I repeat myself every year, but he is truly the joy and the light of our lives.
>
> We pray for you and your life, asking God to give you his protection and keep you in the palm of his ever-loving hand."

We accelerated through daily routines, years of school, camping trips, visits to family, exciting vacations, and all that encompass a generally normal life. Our existence as a trio was close-knit and full of love and laughter.

There have been challenging barricades simultaneously blocking the road. Austin was diagnosed at an early age with ADHD, later to be linked with dyslexia, central processing disorder, and an autism spectrum disorder. Academics were difficult for him. He struggled each year to keep up with the rigor of the curriculum, despite being given support in the classroom. We spent many evenings in tears as we gave our best efforts to affirm his strengths. Teachers were rarely sympathetic. Peers often could not identify with him. We watched his confidence wane as despair settled in.

Our family decided to homeschool Austin. I was a teacher at the time, and I resigned from my position to follow my heart. Those were the best years of our lives. Homeschooling gave Austin the freedom to learn at his own pace and style. Schooldays rarely looked traditional. Austin thrived on being able to do his work in the most unconventional spaces. His favorite place to read was sitting on the back of a horse at a friend's barn.

We called it the "Liberation of Education" for our family. We met all the regulations and created his transcript according to the state requirements. It continued to be successful until he graduated. While this was a perfect fit for Austin, I learned some important truths for my own career in education.

As I returned to work as a classroom teacher, I had realized one majorly important principle: Every student has value and worth. Each one is created uniquely with passion and purpose. Just as I had leaned into adaptability with Austin's learning, that same determination will continue on that trajectory with flexibility and grace. I purposefully stand to truly see each student as an individual who is exceptionally talented with intentional character and gifts.

Parenting continues with its mountain top experiences and deep valley episodes. We rely on our strong foundation of hope and faith to carry us through to our goals and ambitions. Our family continues to draw encouragement from each other as we face circumstances together. No two days are ever alike, but there is a common denominator that keeps us moving forward.

I often wonder how some people can seem to experience an abundance of joyfulness even through difficulties and extreme challenges, while others struggle to find simple joy no matter how hard they try.

How many of us eventually just give up the search and accept that we were passed by when joy was handed out? I believe that my joy is not from the perspective of an annoyingly peppy, happy-go-lucky person who never experiences heartache or grief. I have my share of days, even months, that test my limits and leave me feeling over-anxious and empty.

I've discovered that joy—I'm talking REAL joy, authentic joy—is not a feeling, nor does it come without discipline. It is not about your happiness or the circumstances in life. Nor is it about overlooking and omitting the ache, sorrow, or suffering in living. Instead, it comes from those things.

Authentic joy is pretty darn long-lasting and dependable. It's not likely to give way when knocked around. It's solid and stable.

Sometimes it is difficult to define in just a sentence, yet it is so simply uncomplicated. For me, joy is a strong, heartfelt emotion of radiant satisfaction and a source of peaceful strength. It has become a movement from my soul that I want to radiate to others.

Joy can be present during times of hardship and pain. You see, when you are going through challenging times, it's not possible to remain happy. Happiness is a fleeting feeling. Your external circumstances cast a looming cloud that won't allow it.

You can choose to have joy with internal hope. You have the permission to grant yourself empathy and prioritize those things in your life that bring your heart peace through life's havoc and harmony. It is powerful enough to redirect your course.

Let's step back to the road map and the GPS. If we had to decide which was easier to use between the two, I believe most of us would vote for the latter. A device to show us our next steps with a friendly voice that never shows frustration or makes us feel like failures. Easy is not always best.

Think about just how many incorrect turns we made before the GPS appeared on the scene to save us from lost wandering. I suppose that is a good thing. But isn't wandering a crucial part of the journey? All of these detours have led us up to this point. Even the washed-out, cracked, flooded roads that need repair are important to the journey.

Lean into using that road map with all of its well-defined complexities. Allow the brokenness to build something stronger. We can continue to seek ways to reconstruct our lives in working order.

Without a doubt, I can humbly say that the path I have been on is well-worn, yet beautifully preserved and still a viable route.

With joy.

ABOUT THE AUTHOR:

Social Media:

IG @jilliande

FB @jilliandee

Email jilliande412@gmail.com

Jillian serves as an elementary educator in Clearwater, FL. She has been in the field of education for over two decades. Her passion is to infuse joy to those in educational leadership by focusing efforts on listening, serving, and growing alongside colleagues and friends. She uses her voice to foster hope for equity and empathy.

She is a children's book author and illustrator of *Liv's Seashells, Road to Awesome: A Journey for Kids,* and *Look at YOU, Piper Lou!,* and is the Chief Optimistic Originator of **Imparted Joy, LLC**, her publishing imprint.

Jillian believes the creative process of illustrating children's books brings JOY to life. The expressions, characters, and simple sketches enhance writings with warm emotion as they visually serenade the viewer into the story. The mission is to provide a meaningful experience on every page that captivates the heart.

Each day is a FRESH opportunity to listen, be slow to criticize, and be quick to empathize. Keep dancing and dreaming with JOY.

WHAT'S LOVE GOT TO DO WITH IT?
Julie Nee

You are reading this book for a reason. Perhaps you want to be encouraged, inspired, or impacted in some way by the content within these chapters. I want that for you too, and in that spirit, I want to talk about love.

Love for yourself.

Love for others.

Love for what you do.

Our impact flows through the world as one giant ripple effect. Imagine a ripple that starts at the very center of your heart and pushes its way out into the world--one action, one choice, one behavior at a time. Every action we take fuels our ripple.

It all starts with you. Your full heart, your positive attitude, your encouragement, your belief—they are all catalysts for action. But what about when your heart isn't feeling loving, full, and ready to feed others? If you want to positively impact others, you must be able to pour into yourself first.

I would imagine that you've heard these sayings a few times "you can't pour from an empty cup" or "put your oxygen mask on before helping others." Do you know why they have repeated over and over and over again? Because they're true. So many of us love to do things for others, but when it comes down to saying yes to ourselves, we fail. I've learned the hard way that loving yourself is where it all begins.

When I was going through my breast cancer experience in 2019 (mastectomy, five-and-one-half months of chemo, thirty radiation treatments, etc.), people near and far showed so much love and kindness. My closest circle sat with me during chemo, came to visit from afar, shuttled my kids around, and my husband even shaved my head after my hair started falling out while my kids and sister surrounded me in support. Even with my closest friends and family, I resisted the offers of help.

"I can go to chemo alone. I am fine."

"No, we are good—you don't need to take your time to make a meal."

"I can make the coffee."

"I will walk the dog."

Stupid stuff.

I had to step back and learn to let people show their love by helping. I learned to say yes to them because it was a yes for me. Was it easy? No. Did I do it anyway? Yes. What I know now is that when people want to do something for us and we push back or resist, we are robbing them of the chance to give us a gift they really want to give. The added benefit of allowing people to help you is that you protect your energy so you can do all the things you want and need to do, for yourself, for others, for your business.

What does giving love to yourself look like? To start, it's speaking to yourself as if you are your own best friend. It's encouraging yourself, believing in your potential, and making time to nourish your body so that you can truly flourish.

Earlier today, I pulled an activity card from an inspirational card deck, and it suggested that I make two lists. On the first list, I had to name five things I am grateful for most. Easy! On the second list, I had to name five things I love about myself. Hmmm—a little bit harder. Would it be hard to list five things you love about your best friend, your spouse, or your kids? No. Then don't make it hard to believe in all the goodness of YOU.

Think about things that nourish you and energize you and do more of those things. Also, reflect on the things that deplete you and, whenever you can, remove those things from your calendar and your life. For those of us who love to do things for others, here's the double win; when our cup is full, overflowing even, we have plenty to pour into others to create the positive ripple effect we are striving for.

Our everyday behaviors matter more than we might think. I remember the day I found out I had breast cancer. I had an appointment where my doctor shared the news, and instead of going home, what did I do? I did life as we all do; I had kids to pick up at carpool, groceries to purchase, clients with which to connect. I prayed that the kids, the checkout person, and the clients would be kind that day because I felt like the tears might start flowing with the slightest push.

How many people are feeling exactly that way right now? Is it possible that someone's behavior might trigger an explosion in you because you are tired, stressed, angry, worried about a diagnosis, sick, sad, or upset that you can't control the world? Everyone puts their mask on every day as they go out and engage in the world, and I'm not talking about the kind we wear to protect ourselves from a pandemic.

Here's what you can control: your response to all things, good or bad. You can bring your intentional kindness and light into a dark world.

My neighbors and extended friends made me so many delicious meals and sent lots of flowers and gifts. People who were mere acquaintances came out of the woodwork to show that they cared. It makes me wonder: why do we wait for something bad to happen to do something special? It doesn't have to be a casserole or a flower delivery. For me, both then and now, one of the best things to receive is an unexpected card, text, or phone call.

How can we, everyday people, have a positive impact on the world and influence others? It's doing small things for a big impact. What are some things you can do to create your own kindness ripple? These are some thought starters, but there are so many more. Let your creativity go wild!

- Give a compliment.
- Write a note of encouragement.
- Give something away that someone else could use or appreciate.
- Reach out to someone you haven't connected with in a while.
- Notice and be curious about how others are feeling.
- Ask questions, and truly listen.
- Cook or bake something for someone.
- Share your natural gifts. Draw a picture, paint a rock, record a song, write a poem—whatever makes you unique.
- Serve in your community.
- Smile in-person, online, and behind the mask. When you smile, your brain releases endorphins, and when someone smiles at you, your reward center is also activated. A win-win!
- Choose and deliver a random act of kindness every day; this will make others feel good and will make you feel good too!

You might be thinking that all of this sounds too simple, but that's where the power lies. Your influence ripple comes from the small actions you take repeatedly that deliver a big impact.

Another huge lesson I learned during cancer is about knowing your purpose, in this case, my life and career purpose. I had been speaking and doing workshops on positivity, energy, and mindset for about four years when I learned of my diagnosis. We (Jon Gordon and I) were just about to launch our first big public leadership training event right around the time my mastectomy was to be scheduled. I am so passionate about this work, and I knew I needed to be there to co-lead this training with Jon.

Okay, I really didn't need to be there, and he was happy to handle it on his own. But I wanted to be there, and I needed it for myself. We had been working so hard and planning so long to get to this point, and I didn't want to miss it. My surgical oncologist said that without any complications, I could travel two weeks after the surgery, there was just one rule, no lifting anything heavy. I could do that.

I had a small window of time that the surgery could be done, and it took some major coordination between two surgeons and the hospital to get it all together, but with some frequent connection and follow-up with the scheduler, I got the surgery scheduled exactly two weeks before our event. Whew! Two weeks later, I was co-leading this training in Florida to a sold-out crowd and loving every minute of it.

Time and time again, I would bring my calendar with me to my oncologist, surgical oncologist, and radiation oncologist appointments (who knew there were so many different ones?!). Each time, I would say, "I have an event I want to do here. I have possible travel there. Can we work around this? Can I shift that?"

They thought I was crazy, and so did my husband, but honestly, the work gave me something to look forward to rather than feeling down. Having the opportunity to do work that I love and that I am meant to do is how I got through the hardest days.

During chemo, I had to cancel quite a bit of travel because of my weakened immune system, but I still had local events. I remember one event in my hometown of Charlotte, NC, and it was the day after chemo. I felt so horrible, and I was fearful that I couldn't do it; Jon encouraged me and reminded me where my strength comes from—my inner strength.

I led the training event and didn't even tell the client about cancer or chemo until the end of the day when everything had gone wonderfully. They were amazed and inspired that I still wanted to work this hard and could bring so much energy in the midst of fighting cancer.

My team called me bionic, but doing this powerful work sustained me. Not only did I get to continue making a difference for others all the way through, but because there were some very hard days, I had to regularly practice what I preach. I teach about mindset, positivity, attitude, and energy, and I needed to apply the lessons to myself.

I allowed myself to feel the negative emotions instead of suppressing them. I came back over and over to gratitude. I forced myself off the couch and took one step at a time toward more outside walks, more water, more connection with friends, more sharing, more meditating.

Now it's my turn to pass on the gift of love, empathy, and kindness. I have talked with so many other women who are going through cancer (I hate that there are so many who have to go through this). I can give a true empathetic ear and share all of the very real things about what to expect, how it might feel, and some ways to make it a little bit easier. I remember what it felt like for me when I had a friend to cry with when my hair started falling out. It meant everything to me.

I leave you with this: choose to bring your love and kindness to every interaction, every day, and know that your ripple is extending to places beyond what you can even imagine.

ABOUT THE AUTHOR:

Social Media:

IG @julienee108

FB @julie.nee.7

Email julie@julienee.com

Julie is a leader, motivator, and a passionate teacher of all things positivity. Heart-centered leadership and enthusiasm are her trademarks. She brings a high level of energy and passion to every group she engages. Julie weaves personal anecdotes with relevant calls to action for each specific audience.

Julie brings twenty-five years of business experience in Sales, Sales Leadership, and Marketing, including nineteen years at The Hershey Company, building business, leading teams, and developing people. This experience is the foundation for connecting and engaging with clients around their real business challenges and opportunities. Julie has worked with clients across a wide variety of industries to drive positive change into their organizations.

In addition to keynote speaking, Julie leads the Training team at The Jon Gordon Companies and is the co-creator (along with Jon Gordon) of The Power of Positive Leadership training program. Julie focuses her sessions on helping each organization, team, and individual build more positive minds, teams, and cultures.

WHAT CAN YOU LEARN FROM YOUR FRIENDSHIPS
Jesi Stracham

"Each friend represents a world in us, a world possibly not born until they arrive, and it is only by this meeting that a new world is born."

— Anais Nin

I never was a girly girl. Glitter and frill weren't for me. I'm more of a dirt, grease, and skinned knees type of girl. Because of this, I naturally had more male friends than female friends. I'm not sure if it was due to my paraplegia or my maturing, but something flipped. I wanted to make more genuine female friends with similar interests.

One of my closest guy friends is a fella named Taco. We have traveled the east coast together heading from race to race, making many bro-type memories. Taco is a connector or someone that knows many people. I've built countless relationships because of Taco, but my favorite has to be Jamie.

Jamie and her husband, Jimmy, moved to the Charlotte area in early 2018. We met at an arena cross race. Being new to the area, she was looking to make friends, and I was stoked to meet someone with similar interests. I slid into her Instagram Dm's saying something along the lines of, "Hey Girl! I know you're new to the area and could use some friends here, and I'm looking to make female friends! Let's hang out!" We swapped numbers and made a doggy play date for our dogs Roxanne and Marley at the local dog bar.

I quickly learned that Jamie is a powerful, badass girl boss. A Canadian immigrant, she learned how to do touch-up paint on cars, now building her own company in the states. On top of that, she managed her husband's race schedule, the house, his merchandise line, and her health and wellness. She gave me my first glimpse into what it meant to be a powerhouse of a woman.

My mom always told me that in life, you will come across a few people who are one-of-a-kind in their compassion, authenticity, mannerisms, and overall existence. Hold on to those people tight, as they are few and far between. Jamie is hands-down one of those people. She has taught me so many lessons in our friendship and continues to teach me many more. I want to share some of the most impactful wisdom she has passed to me.

1. Food is Power

Jimmy has Lyme disease. Something that always set his symptoms off was certain foods like gluten and dairy. Jimmy did an extensive elimination diet to find out what food-sensitivities were triggering the disease. I never thought of food as more than nutrients to help us function. Quality, quantity, and how the food is made were factors I never considered concerning my bowels, bladder, or pain. I began to do the elimination diet for myself. I found out that high amounts of dairy caused nerve pain and bowel issues, high amounts of wheat caused bowel issues, and processed foods and sugars caused nerve pain! When I was initially paralyzed, I was told I would have nerve pain and bowel issues because "that's just how it is." I was given a pharmaceutical aid to combat the symptoms. In reality, the food I consumed caused a lot of my issues. We don't know what we don't know, but food has power. What we fuel our body with supports how it functions, both in the short term and long term.

2. "It's not a bad life, just a bad moment."

When the chaos of life would come crashing down on me, Jamie emphasized this. When it feels like I'm being sucker-punched from all angles by life, I think back to when I first woke up in the hospital after my accident. I was terrified, unsure of how my life would look. I can one hundred percent say that I could never predict to be living the incredible life I am living now. Just because things look grim at the moment, doesn't mean they will stay that way. Just as good times don't last forever, neither do the bad. Today's circumstances are not permanent to your tomorrow. Jam helped to solidify this belief for me.

3. It doesn't matter where you come from, or your current circumstances, dream BIG, work hard, & HUSTLE.

Jamie grew up racing dirt bikes across Canada with her aunt and uncle, whom she gives a lot of credit to who she is today. There's no telling where she would be if she didn't have them to guide her. When Jamie met Jimmy, they had a long-distance relationship with her living in Canada and him living in the states. Could you imagine dating someone from another country? After a couple of years together, Jamie moved to the states, learned how to do touch-up paint with a friend, and began working in the field. She then applied for her American citizenship. Waiting patiently for her American citizenship, she was unable to travel back to Canada to see her family for almost two years! She managed to stay positive while building her business, relationship, and life in America. Jamie showed that if you struggle through the trenches and continue to work hard every day, you can live the life of your dreams and then some.

4. Don't partake in gossip or bash others.

The first time I was trash-talking someone to Jamie, she said, "Jes, I don't want to hear it." Jamie doesn't believe in gossip. She emphasized that others' lives are not ours to judge. We have enough to worry about in our own lives. These are still such powerful words for me. In a world full of people that will be fake to your face, then stab you in the back later, Jamie refused to partake. She re-routed any conversation that was trashing someone. She also emphasized that if we focused on our own lives as much as we focus on how others are living theirs, we could live much fuller lives.

5. Control what you can control; don't let the uncontrollable control you.

I used to have a habit of worrying about things at the first sign of distress. I think back to my bladder. I had this wise idea to stop taking my bladder spasm meds for a year. During this time, I could drink around twelve ounces of a drink before my bladder would spasm and I would pee myself. In one year, my bladder shrunk significantly. The urologist urged me to start taking the medication and to consider Botox injections to attempt to expand my bladder. If they couldn't get it to expand, I would need surgery. I was terrified. I panicked. When I took my worries to Jamie, she spotlighted that I didn't need surgery at that moment and to change what the doctor recommended. Humans in general often become caught up by their problems and struggles, allowing them to control their entire existence. In reality, we allow our problems to become the entire situation, masking the good in our lives.

6. Don't settle for less than you deserve.

Don't settle in your career, relationships, or life. I was in a relationship with a man who wasn't anything I wanted to be with. He wasn't a bad guy or anything. He just was not the guy for me. When we first started dating, Jamie told me this point-blank. She said, "I hate to see you settle for less than you want or deserve." Eventually, when I would complain, she stopped me. She said, "If you aren't going to do anything to change it, I don't want to hear about it."

After the relationship ended, she echoed that I should never settle again. She also made me realize how much I settled in my friendships post-paralysis. In the house Jamie and Jimmy rented, I couldn't get into the bathroom. The door was too narrow for my wheelchair to fit. I would transfer to the floor, scoot to the toilet, then transfer up to the toilet. From there, I would transfer back to the floor, across the bathroom floor, and back into my chair. The day Jamie and Jimmy bought their house, Jamie had me come over to make sure the bathroom door was wide enough for me to get in. She was fully prepared to remodel the bathroom if it wasn't. She also had purchased a ramp within two days of purchasing their home so that I wouldn't have to be carried in.

For my twenty-eighth birthday, she planned a surprise party for me, even going as far as to scroll through my Instagram to see who I was close with. She reached out to my friends she had never met to invite them to my surprise party. I never had a friend go so above and beyond to make sure I was included or make me feel so special and valued. After my spinal cord injury, I would isolate myself from anything that made me feel disabled. This includes visiting my friends with inaccessible houses. Jamie recognized this, going above and beyond to address it so it wasn't an issue.

7. Everything will work out the way it's supposed to.

I've met two people in my life that truly lived what's meant to be, will be. Jamie is one of those two people. Regardless of the situation, Jamie approaches it with a smile and the attitude that what's meant to be will be. If something doesn't work out, it wasn't meant to be. If it does, it was meant to be. No-fuss, no fluster. I am working to adopt this mentality wholeheartedly.

8. Give it all to God.

Before becoming a paraplegic, I didn't believe in anything— no higher power, no source, no God. The day before my accident, I was at a friend's grandmother's funeral. As the pastor was speaking, I felt a calmness come over me. I knew everything was going to be okay. The next day, I was in a life-changing accident that left me a paraplegic. I saw my grandmother.

She told me, "Jesi Mae, it's not your time. You can't come with me, and I can't stay with you. You have people to get back to and things to do."

I fought my faith the first few years of my injury, still living a life unguided by faith. I watched Jamie's faith begin to strengthen, and it encouraged me to strengthen mine. In July of 2020, I gave my entire existence to the Lord, asking him to show me my purpose and give me the strength to fulfill that purpose. Having a friend that also put her life in God's hands and guidance helped me strengthen my faith significantly.

My entire life, I've had a lot of friends, but never close adult friends, and surely none that would go above and beyond just for me to be able to hang out with them. Jamie is the friend I never knew I needed. She has so many qualities I work to embody in my own life. She gave me the confidence to realize just how powerful I am. She helped strengthen my relationship with God, and she made me reassess who and what I spend my time and energy on.

We deserve more than we settle for. We can learn a lot from who we surround ourselves with. We learn lessons from their examples, both positive and negative. Jamie made me realize how important it is to have people who add value to your life. She also made me realize what value I bring to others' lives.

Who's Jamie in your life?

ABOUT THE AUTHOR:

Social Media:

IG @jesistracham

FB @jesistracham

Email jesistracham@gmail.com

Jesi Stracham is a trauma survivor on a mission to help individuals see the opportunity in their obstacles. She is the founder of Wheel With Me Foundation and the owner of Wheel With Me Consulting. She's a speaker and a fitness and growth coach. Through her struggles, she works to teach individuals the power of our mindset. Jesi is an honest, authentic, America-loving athlete.

In January 2015, Jesi was the passenger on a motorcycle when it collided with a car. She woke up a week later in an intensive care unit without the use of her legs secondary to a spinal cord injury. Instead of accepting the disability, she rejected the prognosis that she would be wheelchair-dependent for the rest of her life. In the face of adversity, Jesi is recovering from her disability, using it as a platform to reach her world. Since the onset of her injury, she has achieved more than she previously dreamed possible.

Over the past several years, she has generated a significant following among both the spinal cord injury and able-bodied community. Her goal is simple: show the world there is an opportunity in their obstacles, restoring hope during life's difficult moments. She helps people achieve their dreams through the importance of goal setting, taking control of what we have control over, and showing what YOU are capable of with consistent hard work.

MY VILLAGE OF IMPACT
Jessica Perez

Let me take you on my journey of impact and influence that began fifty-four years ago in a little ranch-style home in Tampa, FL, where the African proverb "it takes a village to raise a child" was truly embraced. My parents were high school sweethearts of similar yet different backgrounds raised by a village; cousins, aunts, uncles, grandparents, and great-grandparents all lived within blocks of each other to guide, influence, and love the children as they grew. The philosophy was passed on from generation to generation and was instilled in me as a young girl and blessed to be born in a time when kids could be kids: playing in the street, walking to school, and riding bikes to the neighbors.

The best place to start is by sharing a bit about both sets of grandparents and my maternal great-grandmother who welcomed this spunky, little peanut (yes, I was littler than most at 4'11" in sixth grade and still today) into the village by encouraging, supporting, and cheering my every move. Their unwavering desire to see me succeed in all I chose to do has been a driver for me as I hear their voices in my ear even though they have all passed on.

My dad's parents lived close and were active in my school and sports life. They attended every game, school function, and birthday. Abuelo Kino was quiet, calm, kind, and oh-so generous, while his wife Abuela Molly was bold, adventurous, independent, and oh-so opinionated. They made quite a pair, and each of them developed a key component to my quest to impact and influence. Abuelo Kino taught me to serve, and Abuela Molly taught me to lead.

My mom's parents lived in Orlando for most of my childhood and then moved back to Tampa after my grandfather retired. Their love was big, and the laughs we shared were immense. Abuelo Emilio was boisterous, brave, full of life, and oh-so-fun, while his wife Abuela Beba was quiet, proper, sweet, and oh-so-nice. They, too, made quite a pair. Abuelo Emilio taught me bravery, and Abuela Beba taught me compassion.

My Abuelo Emilio's mom, Ana, was my great-grandmother, whom we all called Abuela Tata. She was the matriarch who was a true survivor. She celebrated her birthdays with me until she passed at ninety-two when I was sixteen. She was strong, independent, always kept family first, and was oh-so steadfast. Abuela Tata taught me independence.

Now let me take you back to that little home in Tampa with a mom who is still impacting and influencing me daily and a dad who passed way too young but is still a driving force in my life. You see, my mom, Maggie, is most definitely the best mother ever. I'm truly blessed to have her be a part of my village that raised me to become the woman I am today. She is a determined energy raiser, a family person, and the youngest eighty-something-year-old woman I know. She worked her entire life while raising my sisters and me alongside my dad in a time when so many women were homemakers. Her work ethic inspires me and has influenced many of my career paths, including the one I am on today: entrepreneur, network marketer, and inspirational speaker and coach. My mom is my catalyst.

My dad, Jack, was quite the opposite of mom. They connected on what matters most: family, faith, love, and sports. He was the reason I became an athlete at the age of five despite my size. He always said that it was the heart of the athlete that mattered, not the height. He passed away when I was twenty-five, at a time when we really needed him to be present as my older sister was pregnant with her second daughter. His gifts were many: loyal, connector, coach, family-motivated, and oh-so detailed. To all who knew him, the list could go on, but to me, my dad was my connector.

In that little home, there were also two sisters: one seven years older and the other one-and-a-half years younger. The three of us are so different yet so the same. The oldest, Jennifer, was more than a sister growing up because my parents worked so much so that they could send us to a private Catholic school. Huge sacrifices had to be made, and our big sis stepped up as a second mom to little sis, Janet, and me.

My two sisters have had a massive impact and influence on my life. They are independent, amazing moms who have raised incredible children while impacting and educating hundreds more as early education teachers, nannies, and even serving as charter school founders. Jennifer is loving, spiritual, always seeking growth, gentle, and oh-so grateful. Janet is funny, nurturing, caring, hardworking, and oh-so creative. My sisters have truly inspired me to give back, to impact the world on a larger scale, and to guide others because we have done these things for each other. Jennifer taught me to be a life-long learner, and Janet taught me to be creative.

From that little home to my first experiences in a structured school setting is where the village began to grow outside of the family to include teachers and coaches. The one with the most impact of influence was my physical education teacher and sports coach at Incarnation Catholic School, Mrs. Sharon Slowey. She was a true example of a stern, fair, loving, knowledgeable, and caring mentor. As the smallest kid in every grade, she always told me I could do any sport I wanted and provided me with the fundamentals that I so desired to be the best I could be. She passed in 2020, but her legacy lives on in me and the thousands of students that she coached. Mrs. Slowey taught me courage.

As I grew into my teens, yet another strong woman entered my village: Ms. Sherry Schaibly. She was named a National Coach of the Year. Ms. Schiably wore mirrored sunglasses and had an awe-inspiring commitment to guide young women athletes to becoming their best selves in sports and life. She continues to impact me with her words of encouragement, her love of family and faith, and her support. Ms. Schiably taught me to be a "Supersizer."

The village continues to grow with the many soul-filling friends and colleagues who have stretched me, challenged me, inspired me, and "supersized me." Throughout my adult years, some of these "villagers" have laid an imprint for a day, a season, or even a lifetime. It's these people that I also give tribute to Heather, Jess, Kelly, Cousin Kimberly, Cindy, Emily, Lynette, Melissa N., Leslie, Brandon, Matty Ice, Tori, Debra, Michelle T, Joanne, Gary, Gretchen, Jess A., and so many more. Part of my hesitation to share these names is that my village is vast and oh-so powerful.

It's the folks that cross our path for a moment that can truly make a difference because they may be exactly what we need to turn a corner, rip a band-aid off, and become more of who we are destined to be. So, for that, thank you to all—Denas, Justins, Brians, Karens, Katharines, Johns, Julies, Leslies, Jasons, Danielles, Amandas, and Ninas—anyone who has crossed my path.

This village of impact has driven me to become a lifelong student, a servant leader, a positive influencer, an energy raiser, and a supersizing catalyst in life and business. My purpose has become the reason I coach, connect, and encourage others in their journeys as we all truly are keepers of our brothers and sisters.

I have begun building a global team impacting thousands with better health and leveraged wealth as I have learned valuable lessons from my village that demand me to share and invoke change. I seek to connect with all those who want more out of life and who are open to the change that is needed to make more happen. Kaizen is a Japanese word that means continuous improvement, which is made up of kai (meaning "change") and zen (meaning "for good"). I intend to live and breathe kaizen as my village tells me so.

Let me leave you with this: who is in the village that has impacted you? I would be so honored if you would take a few minutes to thank the village that raised you to influence and leave the legacy you are meant to leave. To live a life worth living and to leave a lasting impact is the reason why we are all connected. So go ahead: impact, influence, and leave that imprint. You only have one life to live, so make it one to remember.

ABOUT THE AUTHOR:

Social Media:

IG @Jessica_jlo_Perez

FB @JessicaJLoPerez

Email perezjess141@gmail.com

Jessica Perez is a fourth-generation native of Tampa, FL, who still lives, serves, and influences there. She grew up in a very family-centered community that instilled the values of connection, relationships, loyalty, and impact.

After receiving academic and slow-pitch softball scholarships to attend Valencia Community College, Jessica faced a few hurdles that drove her to become the supersizing woman she is today. While enrolling at St. Thomas University with an AA to pursue a BA in Sports Administration, she was offered academic and athletic scholarships once again: this time, it was different.

She had to learn to play fast-pitch softball (they needed her defense) and soccer (a new program that needed players) as she had never played them competitively before; this was the beginning of her journey to take on challenges and grow through them.

Jessica graduated and began her career in education as a Physical Educator/Athletic Director/Coach in private, public, and charter schools for eleven years. She co-founded a Trinity School for Children in Tampa and dove into the non-profit world as a co-founder of CANDO Sports, Inc over twenty-five years ago. She still serves on their board. From education to local government, Jessica began a career with the City of Tampa as Parks and Recreation professional. Her tenure included serving as manager for over two hundred employees, overseeing parks, a marina, community centers, pools, and art studios.

After a great career in both education and parks and recreation, Jessica dove into the world of entrepreneurism and network marketing. She has become a leader in her publicly traded wellness company named LifeVantage (LFVN) and is actively pursued to speak, educate, and lead the charge in growing globally. In addition, she is a certified trainer with the Positive Coaching Alliance and has delivered more than four hundred workshops on the topics of leadership, coaching, and character development. She is much sought after as a coach, consultant, and catalyst for change.

PAGEANTS AND POLITICS
Katie Scott

It was my first time in New York. Like most girls, I dreamt of the Big Apple with all the lights and opportunities. My trip started out just like any first-time tourist. I spent a full day walking to Times Square, eating famous NY street pizza, and having my hair blow in the wind as I rode the ferry to see the Statue of Liberty.

After an exhausting day, we decided to stop into a bakery in Japantown for some caffeine and green tea mochi. My phone was, of course, on the verge of dying, and I decided to plug it into the nearest outlet to let it charge. It was a small place, probably not more than twenty-five seats. I thought I had seen it all and couldn't imagine my trip getting any better. Then walks in Tyra Banks!

Since the age of twelve, when I walked in my first fashion show, I admired Tyra Banks. I even auditioned to be on America's Next Top Model and made it to the semifinals. So, when I saw her, you can imagine how starstruck I was. In my mind she was someone I admired and wanted to emulate, I wanted to be a model and businesswoman just like her. I was so excited, I could barely hold myself back from running over to ask for her autograph, but my friends encouraged me to play it cool. My phone was charging where she was sitting, so we planned what I was going to say and how I would ask for a photograph.

I ran to the bathroom to freshen my hair and makeup. I wanted to look my best when I met my role model. We got our bill, and on our way out, I went to grab my phone. I enthusiastically tapped Tyra on the shoulder and said, "Hi, Tyra! I am a huge fan of yours, and I was one of your semifinalists for this upcoming season of America's Next Top Model!"

She looked over her shoulder unamused, said, "Keep trying," and turned back around.

That was it. I dreamt of the day I would meet her, and this was not what I had imagined and hoped for. I couldn't believe it! I was crushed. As soon as I walked out of the restaurant I immediately began to cry. They say with great power comes influence, and with great influence comes responsibility. Role models play a vital role in influencing and shaping our identity. I vouched that whoever I became, I never wanted to make anyone feel the way I did that day.

I was born and raised in a military family. My father retired from the United States Army as a full colonel. His career was full of incredible experiences, like working as a White House Military Social Aid for President Ronald Reagan and George Bush Sr. My parents met in Washington, D.C., while my mom was working for the FBI. So, as you can only imagine, discipline and integrity were core values that were instilled in me at a very young age.

Growing up, I was involved in everything. I played all kinds of sports, and I even acted in a few plays. I was an adventurous kid who was always ready to try something new. When I was twelve years old, my mother found an ad in the newspaper for an audition for a fashion show. Without knowing any better, I went to the audition wearing low-rise jeans and some cool new tennis shoes. Once my name was called, I walked into a room full of judges and strutted my stuff.

After I finished walking up and down the runway, the director kindly suggested that I get a pair of three-inch heels, walk around the house, do chores in them, and come back the following week to audition again. That day my mother bought me my first pair of heels.

I got home and did as I was told. I walked around all the hallways in my new heels, pretending I was on the runway.

I went back the following week, put on a pretty dress, and strutted my stuff down the runway again, wearing my new three-inch heels. I patiently waited for the call a few days later to congratulate me that I had made the final cut. I had an incredible time at the fashion show, met new friends, and loved being on the runway.

After the fashion show, the director announced he was hosting the Miss El Paso United States Pageant and encouraged everyone to compete. I went from being a 13-year-old tomboy to competing in a major pageant almost overnight.

My mother, who competed in her younger years once for Miss Ohio, was familiar with the pretty dresses but had no idea what all competing might entail. After all, things had changed since she competed. My parents went all out. They spent hundreds if not thousands of dollars on my competition gowns, entrance fees, transportation, training, jewelry, and tickets for all my family to come to see the pageant. But pageants aren't just about who has the prettiest dress; the winner has to have the overall package.

A lot of people don't know this, but when you enter a pageant, you are asked to fill out a bio that the judges use as a reference when you go through the interview process. The winner isn't always the prettiest girl or the one with the prettiest dress. The winner has to have the best overall package. Questions include: What are you doing for your community? What are your plans in 10 years? What do you want your legacy to be?

Can you imagine answering those questions as a thirteen-year-old girl?

I came out of my first interview crying. How was I supposed to know how I was going to make a difference in the world? Competing in pageants helped me understand the importance of setting goals in life and guided me to work towards becoming a positive influence that other young women could look up to.

As my journey continued, the people around me continued to shape my character and core values. When it came time to find a job while attending college, I knew I wanted to work in the fashion industry. I started working at BCBG Maxazria, a high-end woman's clothing store. I loved working there, but I immediately started slipping into my bad habits. I was ten minutes late for every shift. In my first week of work, I was pulled aside by the manager, and she wrote me up without even a warning for being late. I was so mad. I was convinced I would have to start looking for another place to work.

Shortly after that incident, it was announced there would be a new store manager. I was so excited to start fresh with someone new. Her name was Sharon. She was so confident and stylish. Every time she walked into work, she made a "boss entrance." I looked up to her. She taught me how to talk to people, how to manage relationships with my clients, and how to put together a killer outfit. I enjoyed going to work every day, but I still was facing the challenge of getting to work on time. One day I came in late, and Sharon immediately called me into her office.

"Katie, do you want to be here?" She asked.

Without hesitation, I quickly answered, "Yes! I do!"

She replied, "I think you want to be here too, but if you don't show up on time, I am going to have to let you go."

As simple as that conversation was, I still look back at that moment and reminisce on how grateful I was to have such a positive role model so early on in my career. She influenced me to want to make the change I needed to get to the next level. Sharon was helping shape my work ethic and helping me define who I would be as a woman without me even knowing it. That year, Sharon promoted me to management, and I spent the next three years of my life dedicated to managing that store. Sometimes the power of influence can play a key role in what hones someone into success.

After graduating from college, I was ready to enter the next phase of my life. I had spent three years away from home, missing all the major holidays due to the hard hours of retail, and I made the tough decision to move back. Even with my college degree and years of managerial experience, finding my dream job was nowhere in sight. A reality check quickly set in that having a college degree wasn't going to guarantee me the career I had expected.

I began questioning whether or not moving back home was the right decision. After a couple of months of job searching, I was offered an intern position for a city councilwoman. An intern position? I had a college degree and over three years of managerial experience, and now I was going to work for free for experience? It tested my ego, but I was intrigued by what I would learn and what I would experience. So, I accepted the position.

I quickly learned what a powerful woman I was working for and the impact on people that she had as a public servant. She was the mayor pro tem, and she had the power to impact people to influence decisions and legislation for an entire city. But I also saw how it wasn't always sunshine and rainbows in the limelight. Her name was always in the newspaper headlines, and she was constantly a focal point for the five o'clock news. Every word that came out of her mouth meant something, and every decision she made had some sort of impact or influence on someone.

She taught me how to manage a community. I was in charge of assisting constituents' questions and requests and was responsible for her weekly newsletter and social media. This was before social media is what is today, back when the iPhone 6 just came out. I enjoyed working with people, helping to solve issues happening in neighborhoods of constituents, and finally feeling like I was making a difference in the world. Six months in, I had racked up so many parking tickets from not feeding the meter downtown every two hours that I realized I was paying more to go to work than what I was getting paid! And what I was getting paid at work was a big fat zero dollar paycheck. I was so frustrated that I began to question myself, "Is this the right path?" Maybe it was just time to move on to something else.

I decided to stick with it for a little bit longer. The city representative then asked me if I would be interested in managing her reelection campaign. She knew I had no experience and even said she knew there was a learning curve, but she was confident I was capable of doing the job. That year I knocked on hundreds of doors, planned and organized fundraiser after fundraiser, attended every debate, and shook hands with decision-makers for the city. We won that campaign, my first ever.

What no one will tell you is the struggles women face in industries where females are not well represented. I can remember a debate that my candidate was unable to attend, and I was to go in her place to make a statement on her behalf. I can remember how uncomfortable I felt.

I asked myself: Am I overdressed? Is my suit too tight or too loose? Do I blend in?

After quickly scanning the room, I realized there were hardly any other women in the room.

Since Texas became a state in 1845, 5,444 men have been elected to serve in legislation, and only 179 women have served as of January 2021. That's less than three percent.

I admired Courtney for her bravery and the way she commanded a room with confidence in a male-dominated space. She showed me what it looked like to be a fearless pioneer shaping the way for the next female in her path. Working for her inspired me to want to strive to uncover my true potential, overcome obscure limitations and think of the bigger picture.

After her campaign, my name spread like wildfire, and Courtney referred me to other candidates to manage their campaigns. In short of a year, I went from working as an intern in an industry I knew nothing about playing a key role in helping build city council members, judges, and mayors' campaign platforms to help influence people's votes.

I found my niche in campaigns. I ran all the marketing, branding, logos, literature, scheduled events, and fundraisers. One election, our team was hired to work on a higher-profile government campaign. We spent months working to build it from the bottom up.

In the end, our team was so invested in the campaign we were willing to do whatever it took to get our candidate to the finish line.

In the final weeks before the election, I realized invoices I was submitting for my time and graphics that were designed were not getting paid. I even paid some expenses out of my pocket, but that's what I thought everyone was doing. A few days before the election, I had a conversation with a colleague and found out everyone was still getting paid regularly, but I wasn't. Really? As the only female manager, I began to question why wasn't my team making the same sacrifices? Why was I the only team leader not getting paid? Was my paycheck the difference between winning or losing?

Women are faced with glass ceiling after glass ceiling and put in situations that make us question our value. We are influenced by the limitations that others have set for us. When it comes time to break through those ceilings, we often get scared. We don't want to ruffle anyone's feathers. We don't want to be dramatic. But if you don't try to make a change, what justice are you doing for yourself and women following in your path and the ones after them?

I was ready to make the change needed to once again grow into the next stage of life. I was ready to take control. After a lot of research and careful thought, I decided to create my own marketing agency, View from the Top Marketing. I was now in charge of defining my worth. I was ready to take on my clients and treat people and employees the way they deserved to be treated.

I watched my resume transform into something of which I was truly proud. I went from being a thirteen-year-old girl with no vision of how I could make a difference in the world to my last year competing in pageants placing in the top five at Miss Texas USA in 2018 and 2019 and top five at Miss Nevada USA in 2019. I was proud to finally be able to write on my bio that I own a business, I am a political campaign consultant, I serve as the youngest board member on the city of El Paso tourism board, I have aspirations to one day hold a position in government, and I am an advocate for more female representation.

Success is in the journey, but the reward is in the View from
The Top.

ABOUT THE AUTHOR:

Social Media:

IG @ktscott02

FB @katie.scott.52056

Email katie@viewfromthetopmarketing.com

My name is Katie Scott. I am the CEO of View from The Top Marketing. I am the youngest member serving on the "Greater El Paso Civic Convention & Tourism Advisory Board." I represented the El Paso area and placed top five at Miss Texas USA in 2018 and 2019 and top five at Miss Nevada USA in 2019. I am also a host on an Esports news show, "NACL Knows All," broadcasted in 124 airports to forty million people a month around the world, and I am the face of the Hot Tools One-Step Volumizer.

I created my company in 2016. My clients range from politicians, small businesses, real estate, dental, restaurants, schools, beauty, and personal brands. I create business marketing strategies for companies looking to grow their business. I offer Marketing Consulting, Social Media Management, Branding, Graphic Design, Website Design and Development, photography, videography, and event planning.

I am also the youngest member serving on the "Greater El Paso Civic Convention & Tourism Advisory Board" since 2017. I was just reappointed to this position last year for another two years of service. On this board, we discuss convention development, Broadway shows that are coming to the Plaza theater, hotel occupancy, and tourism development.

THRIVING AFTER LIFE THROWS A CURVE BALL
Kristin Smedley

I was so scared. I walked nervously into the biggest, loudest place I had ever seen. It seemed everyone there knew everyone else, except me. I was afraid to look at them, so I looked at the floor. A knot clenched in my stomach, and I tried so hard to hold back tears.

It was my first day of kindergarten, and we had just moved to suburban Bucks County from Philadelphia. There was only one familiar person in the very large room of dozens of children and adults. It was my dad, and I was holding onto his hand as if my life depended on it.

When the teacher told me to let go of my dad's hand and hang up my jacket, I shivered. My eyes filled with tears. My dad crouched down and got eye to eye with me.

"I can't do this," I said to him quietly.

"You *can* do this," he said.

He held eye contact with me and said in a confident, loving way, "I know you are going to do well here. I believe in you," he said.

He believed in me so much that I took one step toward believing in myself and accepted an offer from another student to show me where to hang up my jacket. Still nervous, I said goodbye to my dad, and he watched me until I went around the corner to search for an empty cubby.

My dad, Rich Schneider Sr., grew up in one of the worst neighborhoods in Philly. He never had the opportunity to finish high school. I am not even sure how much high school he was able to attend; he was more focused on surviving than learning. He was one of eight kids whose parents' income could only support half of that number. My Dad always jokes that in his house growing up, the first one to wake up was "the best dressed and the best fed."

Not only did he have to grow up quickly on the streets of Philadelphia, but at eighteen, he was sent to fight in the Vietnam War and then return home to a country that hated him for it. He suffered post-war trauma with zero resources. Eventually, he was raising five kids on a low income, which reflected his lack of educational opportunities.

At this point in most stories about a man with experiences like my dad, there would likely be a lengthy explanation that would end something like, "No one could blame him for becoming a victim of his circumstances."

But that's not my dad.

Victim is not a word in my dad's vocabulary. In stark contrast, my dad is the epitome of the hero that Joseph Campbell defined. Like all the great heroes in the epic movies we have seen, my dad faced challenges, discovered tools for the battles, found guides to help him, conquered his enemies, and learned lessons that he'd teach others.

He wasn't Indiana Jones seeking treasure or Luke Skywalker fighting Darth Vader, but he did survive an impossible war that thousands did not return home from, fought through a socio-economic system stacked against him, moved our family to a place with better opportunities, and guided all of his children to lead successful lives. He didn't fight with lightsabers or swords; he relied on his faith, grit, optimism, and dedication to give his family and the world his best.

Being that he gave his best every single day, he expected my brothers and me to do the same. He was not the guy you wanted to disappoint, ever. He and my mom worked shifts around the clock to be able to put their children through private school. My dad saw education as a privilege that he did not get to have and the number one tool to be successful. In his view, education was the best chance at having a better life. We were not to take it for granted nor waste a single second of our school days.

I remember one night, my dad was on homework duty. I was in fourth grade and had to write an essay. I showed my dad my work. He got about halfway through and gave me a disappointed look. He made me rewrite the essay at least five or six times that night. He kept telling me he expected better because I could do better. I argued that although it may not have been my best, I was confident it would be the best one in the class. He made it crystal clear that he wasn't interested in how my work would compare to the other students. I was supposed to do my personal best. Always.

When I was in fifth grade, my school started a softball program. I signed up to play, and my dad volunteered to coach. He didn't participate in organized sports growing up, but he had watched enough Phillies games to know how to play. He didn't teach the fundamentals because there were other coaches for that. Instead, my dad taught us core elements of successful teams like confidence, leadership, and cooperation.

We did not have a lot of talented individual players, and many had never even picked up a bat or glove. But my dad knew how to build up each girl on the team, giving them the confidence to build their skills while he taught us all how to play. When practices were rained out, he'd gather our team of very loud eleven-year-olds in our tiny basement to review strategies for conquering different scenarios. My mom popped batch after batch of popcorn to keep us quiet as my dad drew all kinds of scenarios on a large chalkboard.

We learned a lot from my dad about the game, and he pushed all of us to do our absolute best, no matter what. He made it clear that the more talented players had a responsibility to teach and guide the other players. He expected every one of us to improve throughout the season. No matter if you were the star pitcher or worst batter, every girl on the team, was treated equally with kindness and respect, and every player was expected to give the team their best. We managed to win the championship that year. It was my first championship victory, and it was the first-ever for our school.

The following season, I was on the mound pitching against the team we beat in the championship the prior year. I was having a great season until that game. I was causing walk after walk, allowing their side of the scoreboard to increase while ours didn't budge. I was frustrated, angry, and disappointed. I felt like a failure.

I couldn't even look at my dad standing in the dugout. He called a time-out and walked out to the mound. I could feel his eyes locked on me, but I couldn't look at him because I couldn't bear the disappointment on his face.

He spent his minimal free time coaching this team. He juggled time with all five kids and my mom while still squeezing in conversations with me about softball strategies and pitching mechanics. He was giving me his best every day, and this is how I was showing up? My heart sank, and my head drooped with every step he took towards me. When he got to the pitcher's mound, he put his face right up to mine and made me look him right in the eyes.

"I can't do this today," I sulked.

"Yes, you can," he said back sternly. "You are one of the best pitchers in this league."

"I am trying my best, Dad," I whined. "But it's not good enough today."

"I believe you are trying your best. But you are trying so hard to do this by yourself. You are getting nowhere. You are forgetting you have a whole team behind you that knows how to play this game. Stop trying to strike everyone out and instead throw pitches they can hit."

"Let them hit? What?"

"Yes," he replied. "Let your teammates use their talents to make the plays. Rely on them."

I followed his guidance, and my team rallied. It wasn't enough to pull off a win, but it was a lesson I would never forget. In fact, it was a lesson I would end up building my life's work.

As I said, my dad is the epitome of a hero. The coolest and most unique thing about him, though, is that he inspires and guides you to be your own hero, to uncover and step into your unique purpose in this world.

Twenty Years Later: The Curve Ball

I was so scared. I stood at the back of the large room filled with people I didn't know. I froze in fear as I looked at the aisle in front of me that would lead me away from my dreams and into a nightmare. It felt like the first day of kindergarten all over again, only this time, my dad was not next to me, and I was an adult now. I had to decide as to whether or not to step into a situation that seemed impossible.

Just a few months before, I was living the life I dreamt of and planned. I landed the job, married the guy, built the big house, and finally, gave birth to a bouncing baby boy. As my belly had grown with my firstborn, Michael, my dreams for him grew too: baseball pitcher, valedictorian, summa cum laude. When he finally arrived in January 2000, I dressed him up in Phillie's onesies and put little baseball hats on him. I was so, so happy.

Then, just four months into living my dream mom life, a doctor said to me, "Your son is blind."

A sucker punch to my heart.

"There is no hope," he added.

Right hook.

"Will he play baseball?" I asked.

"No," the doctor answered.

Knockout.

My son, Michael, and my second born, Mitchell, have very rare blindness called CRB1-LCA. While they were born with some vision, a lifetime of degeneration happened in a very short time.

They are braille readers and white cane users. They cannot see my smile. They cannot see a baseball flying through the air.

When you hear that your child is blind you have two choices: sit on the bench and hug your kiddo tight or step up to the plate and get them what they need to navigate a world they cannot see. I chose to sit on the bench. I hugged my babies tight and prayed blindness away.

No sight meant no success to me, and it seemed the rest of the world agreed. I cried every day over the loss of the life we were supposed to have. Seeing neighborhood kids walk to school made tears leap out of my eyes. I sobbed, driving past the weekend games at the little league baseball fields.

One day, when Michael was barely three and a half years old, I was in the pit of sadness, sobbing over lost dreams and fearing what lay ahead.

He bounced into my bedroom and excitedly said, "Mommy, isn't this the best day ever?" He rattled off the simplest of things— sunshine, his toys—that were making him happy.

The realization slammed my heart. I was paralyzed by fear, anger, and disappointment. Yet Michael was happy, excited, and figuring out how to do everything he wanted to do. The only thing, the only person, standing in his way and his brother's way at that point, was me. I was failing as their mom.

I had been praying the barriers of blindness away, yet I was the one barrier standing in the way of my boys living their purpose. I had been blind to the possibility of my sons having amazing lives, and that blindness was preventing them from accessing the tools they would need to succeed without sight.

I was allowing the world's story of blindness—loss, sadness, devastation—to dictate my story and my sons' stories. I was far from the hero's journey that my dad had taught me to live. So, I thought about what a hero would do: find the tools and guides to conquer the challenges.

It wasn't easy, but I made a choice that day and created a plan to guide my sons. Ultimately, I did what my dad taught me way back on the sixth-grade softball field. I built a team that I could rely on and could help me guide my sons towards the fulfillment of their purpose. I fought through fear, left sadness on the sidelines, and swung for the fences. I ditched my dreams for my boys and instead committed myself to getting them what they needed so that they could achieve their own dreams.

The first step I took in building a team to support my sons was showing up in that room I mentioned earlier and walking down the aisle I was so afraid of at first. It was a conference for people that have blindness as my boys do, and I ended up meeting people that catapulted our journey toward thriving.

The concepts my dad taught me on the pitcher's mound, in stories he'd tell, and through his own behavior have enabled me to teach my blind sons and my sighted daughter how to navigate challenges and live resiliently.

My boys have beaten every grim statistic in the blind community. They are now in college and have accomplished more than most people their ages. Michael was the high school Commencement Speaker, he released an album in Nashville, and he achieved the President's Award at Penn State. Mitch scored in the top three percent of American high school seniors, was identified as one of the top blind athletes in the country, and hosts a radio show on his college campus.

Best of all, both of my boys were on little league baseball teams in our town. The league made a few simple adaptations that enabled a fair opportunity for them. Through determination, belief in themselves, cooperation, and true teamwork, both Michael and Mitchell won championships on each of their baseball teams!

Changing my mindset from victim to hero was the game changer for me. It has enabled me to not only raise all three of my children to thrive no matter the challenge, but it also helped me tap into my own talents and create a global mission that is changing how the world sees blindness.

It took a lot of courage to take that first step at that conference to learn about thriving with blindness, but I did it. And I keep taking one step at a time, building an effective team to help me. Now, I host conferences, courses, and Zoom meetings. I have created a large online community where people from all over the world have joined a massive team to guide families and individuals impacted by blindness to thrive.

I am incredibly grateful to my dad for inspiring my hero's journey, my children's, and now, all of the families and individuals that we touch in the global movement ThrivingBlindAcademy.org. The statistics in the blind community reflect the victim mindset the world has conditioned us all to have: $31.6 Billion burdens on the nation's economy, a seventy percent unemployment rate, and a thirty percent high school graduation rate. We are tackling those statistics by changing perceptions of blindness and empowering everyone in our programs to ditch the victim mindset and embark on their own hero's journey with a global team to help.

The seven elements of my dad's influence that helped me create a massive impact are:

- Live a life of service.
- Believe in yourself (and your mission).
- Maintain a hero mentality, not a victim mindset.
- Give the world your best every day.
- Don't compare yourself to others.
- Treat everyone with kindness and respect.
- Build a good team and rely on them to support you.

It is my hope you'll take these with you to make your impact on our world too.

ABOUT THE AUTHOR:

Social Media:

IG @KristinSmedley

FB @KristinSmedley

Email kristin@thrivingblindacademy.org

Kristin Smedley is the best-selling author of *Thriving Blind: Stories of Real People Succeeding Without Sight* and *Brilliantly Resilient: Reset, Rise and Reveal Your Brilliance*. A recognized expert in the blindness and rare disease communities, Kristin won the highly regarded Champion of Hope Award and was named an Ambassador for the National Organization of Rare Disorders. Kristin is a popular, in-demand speaker who has been invited to share her message internationally.

As CEO of a global patient organization, she coordinated legislation (H.R. #625) that became the first in US history to be submitted in Braille. Kristin spoke at the FDA to help achieve the first-ever FDA-approved gene therapy to treat an inherited retinal disease in the United States. Her TEDx Talk, book, and international summit change perceptions of blindness and have sparked a global movement, Thriving Blind Academy, solving the unemployment, literacy, and financial crisis in the blind community.

During the COVID-19 pandemic, Kristin co-founded Brilliantly Resilient to help people come through life's challenges and setbacks brilliant, not broken.

Kristin offers coaching programs regarding blindness & disability in Thriving Blind Academy and programs for resilience in Brilliantly Resilient. Her most popular speaking topics shared on stages including TEDx, MEDx, US House of Representatives, National Institutes of Health, Novartis, Food & Drug Administration (FDA), Fox 29 Philadelphia, and World Orphan Drug Congress are:

- Impact of Bias
- Blindness Awareness
- Seeing Adversity as an Asset
- Disability/Inclusion
- Resilience
- Non-Profit/Corporate Leadership
- Inspiration and Motivation
- Women's Empowerment

WHO RAISED YOU?
Maggi Welham

Women breed women. Do they breed perfect women? Wise women? Do they breed independent women? Strong women? Simple women? Weak and mild women? Do they raise women to love them or do they raise women to love?

Women create other women every day. Every day, the choice is there, the minute her child comes into the world. Do I coddle her? Do I make her tough? Do I give her hope, or do I show her and tell her that life is hard? Should I lie to her and tell her gifts to show up magically one day a year and we accept them from a stranger none of us knows or sees?

Fortunately for me, I was raised by a woman who knew no limits. I was raised by a woman who saw no fear. I was raised by a woman who believed she knew best. And she was right. I was raised by a woman who decided she would dedicate her whole life to her children.

Influence is a beautiful thing. Influence can make or break you. The influences we have are ones we cannot always choose. As adults, we have a right, and we have a choice. But as children, it is a gamble. We live our entire lives paying the price of this gamble of who bred us, who raised us, and who gave us our voice.

With my eyes wide open, I see her for all of who she is. All of her is beautiful. Sure, it can be messy. It's not perfect; nothing has been handed to her. She has fought her way to success. And when I say success, I mean absolute success. My mom has always said to me, "I will know if I did a good job with you when I see your daughter." She said, "Show me a gem and I will know I succeeded."

Her insight, her heart, her love, where did this come from? Who raised her? My mom is so wise and has been forever. It always felt like we were cheating life, or like we had a wild card. We were poor, and we were struggling. And yet, our family of six felt larger than life. She gave us so much heart, so much courage, and so much intelligence, it was almost like it was unfair to others.

Our mother loved us. She did not care if we weren't brilliant. She did not care if we were lost. She did not care if we were poorly influenced by others. We belonged to her and she would not let go. She loved us loosely with the tightest possible grip. She let us go, yet found a way to keep us close. Our mother moved mountains to create opportunity. She knew no obstacle and declared us worthy, and with that, she developed endless opportunities.

My mother bred me to be good. I love the word "good." I hear it a lot. You're so good. She showed me the value in goodness and the return fee on placing your heart in the right place. She never wavered, she never left, she never got distracted. NOT EVER. She stayed the course. She lived her life loving and serving her family and giving each one of us purpose. And somehow, she did not define our purpose. She provided us with the autonomy to find our own purpose, but meticulously taught us the value of living and speaking with genuine purpose. May your purpose be ambition, she supported. May your purpose be faith and love, she supported. May your purpose be hard truths and brutal honesty, she supported.

Her life, yet hard, has always been purposeful. Every moment is a lesson, every fight an opportunity, every challenge equated to growth. She was living the life of a person with a full university education, yet she did not have one. She was living a life laughing at others with such book smarts, and yet not a degree to stand on.

She knew better, always, and she sometimes humbly let you know. She was never afraid to let you fall flat on your face so you could learn, and she was there to pick you up and dust you off.

She knows. She knows it all. There's no rock unturned, no question unanswered, no heart untouched. She knows what she is doing.

I have never met a person who knows the truth like my mother. Your truth, my truth, his truth, her truth, their truth, you name it. My mom knows the real truth. She just knows.

And she only wants to help you grow at warp speed. There have been times I have spoken to my mom, and I feel like I have received an entire semester's worth of education in one conversation. This is because I leave with confidence, poise, strength, and love. She does not knock people down to build others up. She simply says the truth, even when it is very difficult to hear.

When I was growing up, my mom was close to her parents. Like many, she asked her parents to help her take care of us some days. My mother's father molested me, hurt me physically, and wounded me emotionally. It was a hard truth that was hidden for many years. Like it always does, the truth came out. My cousins came forward and revealed my biggest and darkest fear in life—my mom knowing about her father.

But it came to light. Something I held so deep down, something I tried to bury so desperately was now out in the open, alive and floating around like a foul odor or a dangerous smoke. Lurking about, there it was—the truth—taunting me, poking me, mocking me, there to disrupt and destroy my life. I never thought I could hurt like I did the day I had to confess to my mother that I knew the evil that existed in her childhood home. That I, her baby, knew this pain. I had a story that was so sad in my soul and that I knew would shatter her life.

I told my mother over the phone, as I was away at college in Tennessee. My cousins had told their parents, and they were coming into town to tell my mom. A year before, in a fit of turmoil, I told my sister my secret and admitted my truth. My cousin called my sister to tell her, and my sister began to cry and said, "Hang up and call Maggi."

I hung up the phone with my cousin and knew I only had one option. My mother deserved to hear it from me. So, I called her. She gasped a breath I can still hear to this day and said, "Come home." I rented a U-Haul, packed up all my belongings, and left school. I needed to be with my family. My mom meant for the weekend, but I wanted to be home for, what I saw as a disaster that I had created.

I drove alone the entire twenty-four-hour drive with no music playing and no podcast (it was the 90s). I drove in silence, thinking I have ruined my mother forever. When I arrived in San Antonio, my mother gathered my immediate family for a family meeting. She gave a speech to my family about the courage I had to come forward and how I was going to stand in front of them and tell my story.

I was mortified. I had not shared my story, not like this, in this light, in front of my siblings and my father. I said, I can't, and she said you can, and you will, and my dad said I can't, and she said you can, and you will. She said this did not happen to me. Nothing has happened to any of you. This happened to her, and I am sure there were many days Maggi thought "I could not take this." But she did anyway, so today you will endure hearing her story because you can, and you will.

I stood in front of my family for a while in silence and everyone cried doing everything but looking at me. And then I began to talk, and I stood and I told my story.

That kind of love, that kind of unwavering strength. Where did she get it? Who raised her? How did she know to give me my voice back, to give me my life back? How did she know to create a moment of healing and a genuine circle of trust and safety for me immediately? How did she know to respond with courage, thoughtfulness, bravery, and sincerity?

She knew exactly what I needed in the exact moment when I needed someone to stand up for me, shield me, and protect me. She did it by moving out of the way and making me stand up for myself. She created a platform for me to heal. She got out of my way and out of her own way to facilitate a healing path for me to safety. Not all women can do that. Not all women know how to simply get out of their own way. But the woman who raised me, she knew.

Getting out of your own way is a skill that we as a society have yet to master. I see so many people hesitate, stop in their tracks, run over a concept, run over an idea, run over love because they simply can't get out of the way and allow beauty, love, and success.

In my line of work with high school students, I see mothers like bank tellers see dollars. They are a constant in my world. I see great mothers, I see mean mothers, I see sweet mothers, I see exhausted mothers, I see mothers who think they are failing when they're not, and I see mothers who think they are doing great when they are failing. Being a mother is hard. Being a mother is a special privilege. Being a mother is an enormous puddle of grace. The expectation for motherhood is incredibly unrealistic and hard sometimes. Leading small creatures successfully through life without harm, without tears, without heartache is simply an insurmountable task. Attempting to listen with their ears and not yours, keeping your mind open, but your heart sharp and ready to respond is a challenge. Guard your child, but don't stifle. Nurture your child, but don't spoil. Protect your child, but don't hover. Give your child space, but don't neglect. Love your child, but don't suffocate. There are so many rules. There is so much pressure to create the ideal relationship with your child, where you can say I have provided a good, solid upbringing, I was not part of any demise or an obstacle in my child's success and happiness.

So, what do you do when your child experiences personal trauma? What do you do when you get divorced, and you now have children in two homes? You watch the smallest backpack of life toting back and forth from home to home, with lists and calendars and demands. The rules have completely changed. The parameters, everything I knew, everything I was taught, and the dimensions have changed monumentally.

I am saying phrases that I have never said. I am saying things I never heard as a child, and not only do I not know how to say them, but I also don't know how to feel about the words coming out of my mouth. Please do not forget that you will not be able to call me, and if this happens, I won't be there, and please tell me everywhere you are going and so on and so on. You do it all without mentioning the emotional toll you and your child are experiencing. What am I saying to my children? Are these adult words being spoken to all kids? I would hear people say, your child is so mature, your child is so independent, and all I could hear is you robbed them of their childhood. You forced them to grow up way too soon. You broke them. You bring this beautiful, small, exceptional person into this world to lead, thrive, succeed, and prevail. And suddenly, this person is in a position of pain. Now, what do you do? Who is raising them?

Days become weeks, weeks become months and months become years. They go by, and the time comes for you to remember who raised you. You realize you do not need to be six people to succeed. You can be one and get this done. You can take the family unit values you obtained and apply them to a smaller unit and still be a success. I must remember the talks and remember the love. I must recognize my strength and my power. I can stand up and I can say to myself, you can, and you will.

I will tell my own story this time without the audience, without the assistance of an incredible woman holding my hand, and without my family core, but with the core and family I created. For them, I will honor my mother and I will remember who raised me. I will take all I learned, and I will apply it in the most difficult circumstances. I will take the past and the growth and I will find a way to bring it here, today, to my humans, to my creations, to my home.

I have learned so much through the lessons of my youth and the lessons my adult triumphs and survival have provided me. I learned to be patient and kind. I have learned self-awareness and how to show compassion for others going through loss, whether that loss is death, divorce, moving on, unsettled issues, or the many more obstacles we humans face. I have learned life is messy, and in the journey to find our true selves, there is an absolute beauty.

I have learned to lead people and to parent without the element of fear. I have learned to lead with love and compassion, providing parameters and high expectations without creating a fearful environment. I have learned to appreciate the joy found in discovering my real self and being honest and true. It has given me an obligation to help others find their gifts, their purpose, and their true selves. I love to teach children to have difficult conversations and not run from the truth, especially the truth that lies at their core. I use what I was taught not only from my beautiful, strong, courageous, compassionate mother but from all of life's tumultuous events that have catapulted me to this place. This is the place where growing others is a passion of mine. I strive to influence our youth to be good, honest people who are strong, who can stand up in adversity, and who do not fall for the constant emotional threats surrounding both our youth and adults today.

I was bred to hold a loose grip and sustain a tight hold. I was taught to let go yet stay close. I was taught to communicate love and connect with an open heart and a brilliant mind. I was taught to fight. I was taught to get out of the way and allow growth, love, acceptance, and grace. I was taught to give my all without distraction and to love my family above all.

I will honor my mother and I will remember who raised me. I was raised to be your mother and I will raise you to remember.

ABOUT THE AUTHOR:

Social Media:

Email welhammaggi@gmail.com

Maggi Welham is a mother to son Evan and daughter Kyle. Being a mother is her favorite leadership role in all her career of influence. She has been in education and coaching for almost twenty years. Maggi is a devoted daughter, sister, aunt, coach, colleague, and friend. She spends her time with her family entertaining, reading, golfing, shopping at the Market Square, and playing cards at home with her kids. Maggi shared her story to inspire everyone to live life honestly and unafraid.

FOLLOWING YOUR HEART'S VISION FOR LEADERSHIP
Melahni Ake

What do you do next when something inspires you deep inside your heart?

Do you act on it right away? Do you make an intentional decision in your mind as to when to explore this inspiration deeper? Do you have a journal where you collect your thoughts? Do you have a mentor or an inner circle to express your ideas? Do you find a way to communicate this vision and share it with others?

My story is of significance where God has been the foundation for developing the vision of my heart for leadership over my life. It also includes the steps that he led me through to gain clarity in my purpose, which is now allowing me to make a more significant impact.

My Career
In 2013, I worked at Cook Medical, the world's largest private medical device manufacturer, for almost ten years. Bill Cook, the founder, was a visionary leader who wasn't afraid to collaborate with other thought leaders to create patient-focused solutions in over eleven medical specialties. Bill Cook was eighty years old when he passed away on April 15, 2011. In July of 2013, the Cook Medical

Group celebrated fifty years of medical device influence and the impact in the world; this event was the beginning of a tough time of reflection for me. Anyone that understood the "Cook culture" considered it a privilege to work there. Job seekers and industry leaders would often say, "You can't get a job with Cook Medical unless someone dies. The culture is so great, no one ever leaves." Like many of the other Cook Medical employees, I was in a position to sit back, relax, and enjoy the corporate family culture until I retired. While all of this indeed lined up on paper as a beautiful life and guaranteed retirement plan, I was grateful, not fulfilled. I was forty-five years old, living a successful life, tenured as a sales director, always focusing on ways to add value to physicians and clinical teams as an extension of Bill Cook's vision.

I was being pulled, however, into a need to connect to a more profound inspiration that would require a different approach and different challenges for my life like I had never experienced. I knew this was God pulling on my heart to show me something that was waiting for me; it was something that I couldn't explain. I could only feel it through my heart's vision.

Have you ever been in a situation like this in your life where your life or career is running like clockwork, and yet your heart is tugging on you for change? It was on my heart, yet it didn't make any sense to me. I found myself asking God, "How can I have all of this success and feel like anything is missing? Am I just not grateful enough? Can you show me how to be brave? "What in the world am I thinking, and how can I walk away from this kind of stability into something one hundred percent unknown? *God showed me that I needed to become stronger in my faith.*

Being a natural servant leader is a quality that helps you become successful in your career. In a company, your enthusiasm for serving and adding value to others absorbs your energy into a calling, not just a job. *During this period in my life, my heart was searching for different solutions to make a more significant impact, and I knew it was time to discover more.* The scariest part was how I would know what the right next move was when I had been living out Bill Cook's vision every day. I was so comfortable being a part of the brand that customers valued, and I appreciated being accepted, respected, and valued as well. Yet, I didn't feel that I was living my purpose as God had designed me. Being a person of faith, it seems that choosing to live a purposeful life would be easy, so why did I feel so disconnected from my own life?

Have you ever had sleepless nights feeling like your life or career is a puzzle trying to find the missing piece? Have you ever felt that your heart is breaking because you are suffocating from your desire to communicate and share your vision? Why is it so hard to communicate what we see from our hearts? Why does it take so much time to make an inevitable decision? Is it simply because we are trying to control our outcomes? Do we fear what others think if we communicate our heart's vision? Or is it because our heart sees the potential to make a more significant difference, which scares us?

That's precisely the way that I was feeling, every day. I couldn't explain it clearly to anyone, yet I knew I needed to make a different kind of impact in my heart. I was suffocating, trying to figure it all out on my own.

My Reflection

I remember an industry colleague approached me and asked me to join him in launching a portfolio of new products for their company. As I reflected and contemplated my decision to make a change, my boss told me something I will never forget. He said, Mel, you must make the best decision for yourself and your family. If this is something driven from your heart, it will always work out the way it is supposed to in the end. As I decided to resign from Cook, I took a considerable risk, prayed a lot, and relied on my faith. I knew no matter what God would provide, which gave me the inner confidence to move forward. I knew I was not in control.

What drew me to this organization was the magnetism to work alongside another visionary leader to build a niche market for this organization and create greater brand loyalty. At the height of my professional career, I blended my clinical knowledge and passion

135

for developing people to develop a sales training platform for the domestic and international sales teams. In learning these new technologies, research doctors, and training facilities worldwide, I fed my faith and leaned into the possibilities that God had delivered. Over the next few years, the founder retired, and the vision pivoted from one of servant leadership to shareholder influence; this was the moment when I could feel everything starting to change. What I now know is what I felt was the impact of godless leadership. *The shift in influence changes the shift in impact.* My mentor, Dr. John Maxwell, teaches that "Leadership is influence, nothing more, nothing less" This shift in leadership changed the industry's impact.

During the spring of 2016, I was approached by a coordinator from the John Maxwell Team, sharing information about a new and evolving Personal Leadership Development Certification Program. This organization was responsible for equipping leaders who would become the legacy of the faith-based, global leadership expert himself, Dr. John C. Maxwell.

This conversation inspired the vision in my heart, and I started reflecting on what I was doing in my career and especially in my life. I had taken a considerable risk, leaving my professional comfort zone after ten years in 2013, so why did this inspire me and challenge me to think differently now? I realized it was because although I had challenged myself to grow professionally, I didn't know how to grow personally, and I was longing for a faith-based mentor to gain clarity to create a life of impact. Maybe this was the piece that I had been missing? I knew that I must find a way to learn more about this opportunity.

God inspired me. It was like my heart was on fire. I started making a list of my challenges and the people I surrounded myself with in life. I began to think more into every aspect of what personal leadership growth meant for me. I didn't know all the answers; I only knew the next step. I knew I needed to find a way to make this happen. I knew this was a God nudge.

My Fear

As I started to learn about the financial commitment for the program, I was immediately overwhelmed with fear and unsure of how to make this work. This decision, for me, felt like it could be the missing piece that I had been searching for my whole life. So why couldn't I just let go of the fear and let God help me figure it out? Did I not value myself enough to invest in myself for something I believed would add value to my life? Why was I questioning this decision? What was the cost of something that held such value? What was I willing to invest to receive the value of this personal development community? God was testing my faith.

Naturally, in my current role, I went to my leadership team and announced I was joining the John Maxwell Team, a personal leadership development certification program. Would there be a specific form I may need to use under our professional development tuition reimbursement? I received the following responses: "Who is John Maxwell?" and: "This type of certification isn't covered under a university program, so our assistance programs can not cover it."

I now knew that God was in the middle of the vision he was leading me to, so I prayed about this financial responsibility and the burden that it would place on our household. I chose to feed my faith instead of my fear to help me make the next decision that has ultimately been the catalyst and influence to impact everything else in my life.

My Commitment to Grow

Once I submitted my payment, there was no turning back. I was surrounded with access to mentors and developing leaders worldwide, fielding eighteen coaching calls a week, and was given two tickets to LIVE2LEAD, John Maxwell's signature annual conference for developing leaders. The meeting would be held on Friday, October 7, 2016, in Atlanta, Ga, which was three days before I had to be in Germany to facilitate new hire sales training.

What did I do? I fed my faith instead of my fear. I didn't worry and think about how this event would get in the way of my work commitments or doubt my decision on the timing or fret over the what if's.

Instead, I immediately asked my husband, Joe, for his support to attend the conference with me. We met John Maxwell live on October 7, and then Joe dropped me off at the Atlanta International Airport and drove back home eight hours to Indianapolis. This solution allowed us to experience the event together and fulfill my work obligations in Europe. My husband's support in my journey has been immeasurable. Teamwork makes the dream work.

When you are committed to a plan, and God is in the middle of it, nothing can stop the impact that happens next.

On the first day of the International Maxwell Certification, March 22, 2017, I was ready to grow! John Maxwell challenged us to study his book, the *15 Invaluable Laws of Growth*, as a mastermind, and he gave us precise instructions on the process and how this would ultimately help us improve our lives. I knew that by following his teaching, I would grow. *I didn't know all the steps; I just knew the next right step. I trusted the process.*

INTENTIONAL VISION FROM MY HEART

I bonded with growth-minded leaders and studied the *15 Invaluable Laws of Growth*. I created weekly masterminds on an internet training platform called zoom and stayed committed to my personal development as a significant priority in my life.

Through 2017 I began reflecting on my upcoming fiftieth birthday, Jan 12, 2018, and my purpose puzzle unfolding in front of me.

● What were the lessons I had learned from these fifty years?

● Who were crucial influencers who had impacted my life and my beliefs?

● Who were those that helped me to see others' hearts?

Have you come to a point in your life where you may have asked yourself these same questions?

My Everyday Leaders

My grandparents, Paul and Mae Qualls, were Nazarene Song Evangelists that were fifty years old when I was born, and I reflected on how they showed their hearts through their ministry and their servant leadership every day. They always protected, guided, and encouraged me after my father passed away from lung cancer. They served God's vision and made a significant impact in the world through their ministry.

I asked God how I could impact my life to create significance for others the way my grandparents did? What was my purpose in creating a life of impact? If my mentor was teaching me about influential leadership, I needed to create something to celebrate leaders in the world; people like my grandparents, who followed their hearts by following God's vision for their lives.

Then, it all became clear.

As an avid fan of technology, I asked my husband, Joe, for my fiftieth birthday present to help me create a podcast to celebrate everyday leaders from around the world, and it would be called Everyday Leaders 50in50 (50 Guests in 50 Weeks in my 50th Year).

From my first mastermind in March 2017 to over 20,000 hours in consistently studying, teaching, and coaching personal development leadership principles, I connected to leaders all over the globe.

My personal development includes:
- 500 Everyday Leaders Podcast broadcasts
- Guest on over 200 Podcasts
- Host of three LIVE Leadership Summits
- Four published co-authored books
- MC over 50 Virtual Summits
  - Over 900 consistent days of morning leadership devotionals (join us!)
- Over 25,000 hours invested in personal growth

I am learning to share God's favor in my heart.

In 2020 I became certified with the WHY Institute. As the first US Affiliate Consultant, I help corporations discover persona and professional operating systems through identifying leadership principles.

Learning to see God's plan for your heart is the most important leadership lesson you can learn that will influence your life to make a more significant impact.

If God is nudging you right now, open your heart and receive God's vision for your life. If we learn to practice-listen to God with our heart, our life and the lives of those we love will be impacted in ways that we could have never imagined.

#everydayleaderschangetheworld
#50in50
#theheartofleadershiplive
www.everydayleaders.com

Bonus: Chip Baker was my fiftieth guest in 2018 and still holds such an important place in my heart. I am on a mission to change the world through my vision to impact people's hearts for leadership.

ABOUT THE AUTHOR:

Social Media:
IG @ everydayleaders50in50
FB @ MelahniQuallsAke
Email make@everydayleaders.com

Melahni Ake is the founder of Everyday Leaders Professional Coaching and Consulting is a proven leader in Strategic Corporate Branding, Market Creation and Development for Start-Ups, Leadership Coaching, and Culture Development and uses her training from Walt Disney World to challenge industries to create one of a kind customers experiences that make a bigger impact in delivering value. She graduated with honors from the University of Indianapolis in Business Management and Organizational Leadership and is certified through the John Maxwell Team as a Leadership Coach, Speaker, and Trainer and recently nominated for three John Maxwell Culture Awards, including Modeling Consistency, Allowing Room for Faith and Living Intentionally.

In 2020, she became the first US Certified Affiliate Coach and Consultant with the WHY Institute to assess strategic communication and operating systems for improving personal growth and development as well as professional cultures.

Melahni is the host of Everyday Leaders Morning Leadership Devotionals, Everyday Leaders 50in50 Podcast, Everyday Leaders Annual Leadership Events, Association of Women's Business Owners Board Vice President of Program Development, Top Floor Women-Business and Program Development, Pass the Torch for Women, Legacy Leader and Host of the Torch Talk Podcast, Virtual MC, Voice Actor and Event Host for over hundreds of programs.

You can connect to Melahni at www.everydayleaders.com

HER
Na Tasha Pepper

When I think about the influences that shaped my life, many events and people come to mind. In my short thirty-one years of life, I've experienced and seen so much that it is hard to narrow it down to one. In this chapter, you will take a journey into the experiences that have shaped me into the person I am today, which still affect me as I continue to grow.

It's because of her that I am the woman I am today. It's because of her struggles that I can bear the weight of this thing called life. It's because of her pain that I can face my hardest times and somehow push through (tears and all) as if it were a walk in the park. It's because of her strength that, no matter what adversaries try to deter me, I can put an "S" on my chest and bulldoze through them all.

My life would be nothing without the woman I am blessed to call my mother. I am sure you think this is just another cliché subject to write about. But I am hoping by the end of this chapter, you too will understand why I owe my successes to her.

For as long as I can remember, my mom has been the rock of the family. She is the go-to person for those who call her sister, aunt, cousin, niece, mom, Na-Na, wife, and friend. There is a type of pressure that comes along with this great responsibility, yet she handles it all with grace and poise.

I'm reminded of times growing up when she would sit us down for those talks every child hates. I remember her telling us about her experiences growing up and what she learned from them. She shared these stories with us in hopes that we could learn from them too. As a child, you really don't appreciate those moments, but as an adult, I often reflect on them to help guide me. Oh, how I appreciate them so much now!

I've witnessed her succeed as a single parent, battle depression, push through the loss of loved ones, be abused by the hands of someone who was supposed to love her, and suffer sleepless nights as she works shift after shift to take care of her family. Nonetheless, her love and selflessness never wavered. She never complained. She never showed us her tears. She never showed us any doubts or fears that she may have been experiencing. When hard times came, we never knew about it because Mama was going to make sure her children were taken care of by any means necessary. She'd work job after job, so much so to the point that the only time I would see her was when I was leaving for school.

Her strength and faith continue to carry me through my adult years. My mom birthed me as a teenager going into her senior year of high school. We've always had a roof over our heads, clothes to wear, food to eat, and transportation to get us to where we needed to be. I vividly remember moments in her life that could have broken a young single mother, but she dedicated herself to making our lives better than hers. Now don't get me wrong, we struggled like any other middle-class family growing up in the Midwest, but her dedication made our struggles so much easier to bear.

I participated in almost every sport and extracurricular activity you can think of—cheerleading, soccer, gymnastics, track, newspaper/journalism, student council—without regard to our financial situation. Instead of telling me that she couldn't pay for cheer camps, uniforms, and everything else that came along with it, she pushed me to be all that I could be and to pursue what interests me. There were no limits when it came to allowing her children to explore and grow.

You see, at this time, my mom had five children of her own and raised her nieces and nephew for a few years off and on. At one point, we had ten children in the house. We never missed a meal, birthdays were still fully celebrated, and Christmas was always a joyous occasion for everyone in our home. No one was left out. The strength of this woman is unmatched. The love and selflessness of this woman are unheard of. She is the reason why I am who I am today.

My mom is a firm believer in doing right by others no matter how they treat you. She instilled in us, at a young age, to follow Christ and allow Him to guide our paths. Even when I voiced my indifference as I journeyed through a rebellious period as a teenager, she would continue to reassure me that everything was going to be okay. She respected my thoughts and worries.

At times of pure ignorance, I would call her and tell her that I sometimes hated that she raised us to be selfless and giving because it's easy to be taken advantage of repeatedly. And she told me to keep being generous no matter what. Those words of wisdom still resonate in my everyday encounters.

There is so much I can say about this woman I am blessed to call mother. She is my rock, my everything. She is a jewel that I am so fortunate to have in my life. Through her tests, trials, life experiences, and overall journey, she molded me into a woman that cannot be moved. She raised me to be a self-made person who can conquer anything I put my all in. I am forever grateful for her guidance, love, light, and existence.

I mentioned earlier about a rebellious teenage period; this is no uncommon conversation as most teenagers go through this phase. My rebellion stemmed from many, many experiences that I won't dive into now. One moment I will talk about is the death of my best friend, who I called sister when I was just fourteen years old.

We did everything together. We would stay up all night dancing, making up routines, talking about boys, dreaming about what we wanted to be when we grew up, and so much more. The summer of her death, we worked on a project that would have possibly featured a young artist.

She, too, was very active. She played basketball, ran track, played volleyball, and was on the dance team. We were inseparable. When I got the news that she had been rushed to the hospital due to an overdose, I was shaken to the core. That day she wanted to stay over at my house. Of course, I immediately thought it wouldn't have happened if I had been with her. I beat myself up for a long time with "should have, could have, would have" scenarios.

When I lost her, we still had so many dreams to fulfill. She had gone through a lot in her short life. She was just thirteen years old, but her life experience was not.

As I mentioned earlier, my mom raised me to be a caring and selfless person, so at a young age, I knew I had a gift of influence, and I knew I wanted to help others. The death of my friend encouraged that drive like no other. At fourteen, my life had a new meaning. I knew that no matter what I ended up becoming as an adult, I wanted to connect and touch people in a way that I wish I could have done for her on the day she passed.

I became more intentional with all interactions and sought deeper meanings. I developed an urge to help anyone in need and to listen to those who feel that they do not have a voice. I long to open a center and safe place for young girls and teenagers. So much of what I have accomplished and endeavored in life has been in tribute to my friend.

The lessons from my mother and the untimely death of my friend both shaped me to be who I am. Because of them, I take "no" as a challenge. Because of them, I take failure as a steppingstone. Because of them, I seek to find a deeper meaning in life. Because of them, I do not take experiences for granted, big or small. Because of them, I know that no matter what I have to endure, I will succeed. Because of them, I can stand strong and proud, knowing that my life has meaning. Because of them, I am who I am. Without their influence, I would not be the wife, mother, sister, cousin, niece, friend, entrepreneur, or colleague that I am today.

It's because of HER.

ABOUT THE AUTHOR:

Social Media:

IG @_tweetys_sweeties
FB @npepper90
Email natasha@tweetyssweeties.com

My name is Na Tasha Pepper. I am thirty-one years old. I've been married for eight years and counting to the love of my life (Trent Sr.) and have three beautiful children (Trent Jr., Layla, and Kenneth). I am approaching five years of entrepreneurship.

I own a bakery, Tweety's Sweeties, LLC, where we live by the motto, "Giving your buds MORE than average." We pride ourselves in giving our customers (from the general public to corporate) a memorable experience from the first encounter to the last bite. We've won awards, featured in online magazines/blogs, and hosted many classes teaching techniques, baking, and more. We have been recognized by the Better Business Bureau for our exceptional products and customer service. Our products have also been featured on the news as a part of Valentine's Day promotion in the local area. We are looking forward to expanding our brand and reaching new heights.

"With men this is impossible, but with God all things are possible" (Matthew 19"26 [NIV]).

VALUE: THE UNSPOKEN SUPERPOWER
Nicole Ruiz

Value is almost always associated with money, but how did a simple piece of paper find its value? Looking at a dollar bill, I can see the different shades of green and the worn-out edges. This dollar bill has been owned, traded, stepped on, and crumbled, and yet this dollar bill is still worth a dollar. It did nothing to earn that value. It didn't "find" its value. And yet, because its creator declared its worth, so it is.

You, my friend, are far more valuable than this dollar bill, yet this dollar knows its value. It can never disappear, no matter what. Until the day it is set on fire, it holds value. Do you know your value?

Value is the unspoken superpower that affects every aspect of our lives. How we see our own value sets a precedent that tells people how to treat us, and more importantly, it determines how we show up for ourselves and our dreams.

When I was seventeen years old, I had the vision to launch a clothing line and marketplace for socially conscious consumers. Twenty years later, I finally made it happen. In January of 2020, I was ready to launch my dream. I was waiting for this moment for Twenty years. I had everything right on paper—I had just bought my house, I was with the man I wanted to be with, my savings was exactly where they needed to be, and I had just quit my job. When the time came to launch, I froze. I became scared, lost, afraid, and overwhelmed. My heart was broken. This vision had motivated me throughout my life, and what's worse, I thought it was my life's purpose.

My mind was consumed with negative thoughts. I am such a loser. This is what I wanted. This is what I worked so hard for, and now I can't do this? I am not enough. I don't know what I'm doing; I am never going to make enough money to replace my job. At the time, I wasn't the only voice on the self-sabotage train. My boyfriend at the time said to me, "You can't be a CEO and a mother, or you will be a horrible mom." This was just more "proof" to myself that I couldn't accomplish this dream.

The truth was, I had spent the last fifteen years working for startup companies and launching them. Working directly for the owner and CEO, I had a front-row seat to learn what to do. If it wasn't skilled, and it wasn't money, what was holding me back? I had spent most of my life searching for someone to give me value. I wanted someone to tell me I am enough for my own dreams, for love, for value, and for significance. I was in a constant state of seeking value, approval, and love.

At work, I found myself working from 6 a.m. to 10 p.m., living out of suitcases and in airports. I sacrificed my body by exchanging morning workouts for emails and phone calls. Why? Maybe if I work harder, my boss will see my value, and then I would feel valuable.

I will never forget when one of my bosses said to me, "What does a thirty-year-old woman know that I don't?" or "Why are you cheap, is that because you are Mexican?" I was searching for validation, yet I got devalued based on my gender and race—two things I cannot change.

This value conversation is subconscious. I couldn't see it, but it does exist.

You see, the more I searched for validation, the more I began to lose it.

I thought that maybe if I buy valuable things, then I can feel valuable and show everyone I'm valuable. When that didn't work, I was left with debt. In my romantic relationships, I was searching for my value. I would find myself trying to prove my worth by giving so much. I would ask for a need like a kiss or a hug, and I would be pushed away. I wouldn't say anything, and I would tell myself, "Oh it's okay, that's just how he is." I was denying my own need for love. At that moment, my subconscious was telling me that he is more valuable than me.

I started to build resentment at work, in my relationships, and in my friendships. I wasn't expressing my needs and desires or following my dreams because of this internal battle. In other words, my low self-value temperature was set, and it was affecting every area of my life.

Picture a ball that symbolizes my inner value. Every time I didn't speak up after a devaluing comment or skipped a workout because work was more important, it was a pinhole in my value, again and again.

Back in January of 2020, my internal value ball was as flat as a pancake. Most of my self-worth had escaped from these tiny holes over time when I did not recognize my value.

When it was time for me to choose my value in a big way by starting my own business, I had nothing left for me.

I want to ask you one question: where in your life have you allowed other people to determine your value? Maybe you only feel pretty when your significant other tells you. Maybe a teacher told you that you were dumb, and to this day, you hold that label. Maybe a coach told you that you will never make the pros. Take a moment to feel your subconscious value temperature. Write in a journal where in your life you have allowed other people to determine your value, and how has it affected you?

Next, ask yourself this question: where in your life have you been avoiding choosing your value?

Avoidance is a form of an unspoken value conversation. We hide our true desires because we don't think we are worthy of them.

Here are some examples of this in my life: I have been avoiding having a clearing conversation with a parent and setting boundaries. I have been avoiding distancing myself from conditional friendships. I have been avoiding breaking up with the boyfriend/ or girlfriend that I know isn't part of my overall life vision. I have been avoiding asking for a raise.

Take a moment now to journal. Ask yourself where in your life you have been avoiding choosing your value.

At this point, we have looked at how we allow other people to determine our value and how we avoid choosing our own value. Now, it's time to look inside.

How are you devaluing yourself? Are you devaluing yourself by evaluating yourself against others?

Evaluation by definition is "making a judgment about something." You are either devaluing or validating yourself.

Am I as good as this person? Are they prettier or more successful than me? With this subconscious conversation, we see ourselves based on judgment. When I truly knew my value, the evaluation stopped, and the constant devaluing side chatter disappeared. It is only when I start to see my worth in a new way that I begin to activate new results in my life.

It hit me.

There is nothing you can do, say, create, become, or buy that makes you valuable. There is only one of you!

Really take time to think about that.

The most valuable things are one of a kind. No one will ever think, be or act like YOU again, ever. The rarest things in this world are one of these questions survive. What is our value? How do we gain our value? That is like asking what is the value of the sun? What is the value of the water? What's the value of oxygen?

There is no limit on the value of these things. Without them, we cannot live, just like there is no limit to the value of you! If you are breathing, then you are valuable! Value is your birthright.

That was my Oprah ah-ha moment. Value is my birthright.

So, there I was, ready to "start my life" and "live my dream" and I'm stuck. At the time, I didn't know how to describe it, other than I felt like my feet were in concrete, stuck. That pain was real. Just when I thought it couldn't get any harder, Covid hit. By the time 2021 came around, I was so frustrated and disappointed in myself. I started to understand that I was allowing other people's opinions to define my value. I was constantly communicating in a devaluing way to myself. Then, it hit me—I was making all the pin holes in my own value ball.

We have all heard that the definition of insanity is doing the same thing over and over and expecting a different result. I was ready for a different result. I was ready to do something different.

I started to take action. Action is the key to acknowledging value. To blow my value ball back up, I had to patch the holes. Otherwise, the air would just escape. The patches, or value actions, are action steps that confirm value to yourself!

I'm going to say that again. The patches to the value leaks are action steps that confirm your value to yourself! It's showing yourself you are enough. You are worthy. We go from complaining about it to doing something about it.

From the journal prompts above: Where in your life have you allowed other people to determine your value? How has it affected you? Where in your life have you been avoiding choosing your value?

Make a list that reframes the value leaks by using the following phrase: Because I am valuable, I will _____ by _____.

For example:

(Value Leak) I have been avoiding getting my finances in order.

(Value Action) Because I am valuable, I will call a financial advisor for support by 2 p.m. today.

(Value Leak) I have been avoiding talking to my boss about a raise.

(Value Action) Because I am valuable, I will talk with him tomorrow at 9:00 a.m. Add a time!

Think of all the pillars in your life: relationships, work, finances, health, and body. Are there any other value leaks that get to have value actions? Take this time for yourself and write your value reframes now. There is lightness and freedom in knowing you always have the power and choice to change what isn't serving you.

Taking action is just one way to honor our innate values. The next step is to acknowledge the God-given gifts, talents, and dreams that only you have! What are some of the gifts, talents, and dreams that you have? Are you using them? If not, why not? Notice the conversation you are having with yourself. Are you poking holes, and how can you change the way you are speaking with yourself?

Take a moment and journal now: What are some of the gifts, talents, and dreams that you have? Are you using them? If not, why not?

One of the key factors that hold us back from living our life to the fullest is fear. Fear stops the value action steps from occurring and holds us back. The fear of failure, rejection, disappointment, being made fun of, unloved, cast out, and alone are real, common feelings.

How do we overcome fear? How did I get my feet out of the cement and start the dream I had for twenty years? It took action, and to get to the action, it took courage. Courage is the realization that fear is there, but we do it anyway! It's the reframe.

"I know this may be a bit painful, but it will be more painful to be on my death bed and know I never tried because I was scared. So fear, I know you are there, and I know you will be there. I am going to take this one step towards my goal."

What is the one thing you can do NOW as an action step to get closer to making your dream a reality? (Dream + Value Action) Action steps confirm value to yourself! Take time to write out those first steps. Once you complete the first one, ask yourself, "What I the next step to moving this ball forward?" Add specifics. "Because I am valuable, I will do _____ by _____." Before you know it, you will be on your way to accomplishing your dream.

You were created with a dream, a vision, and a talent that no one else has because there is only one YOU. You are Priceless. Every time you breathe in, remember you are the gift. YOU ARE VALUED, YOU ARE WORTH IT, AND YOU ARE ENOUGH!

One of my favorite quotes I will leave you with is this: She remembered who she was, and the game changed.

ABOUT THE AUTHOR:

Social Media:

IG @nicolecruiz

FB @nicolecruiz

Email nicole@nicoleruiz.com

Nicole specializes in strategic planning of operations, sales, and marketing for startup companies to drive continued revenue growth. Operationally, Nicole has a track record of scaling multiple companies from an idea to hundred-million-dollar evaluations through revenue growth, leading executive partnerships, team building, and brand voice. Nicole works with individuals that have an idea but don't know what the next step is. She will uncover the unspoken block to conquer it and launch that idea into a revenue-generating business. Nicole is a facilitator of workshops on Value, the Unspoken Super Power, and is available for speaking.

Website: nicoleruiz.com

DON'T CURSE YOUR STRUGGLE
Rachel Baribeau

What if I told you that from your greatest pain can come your greatest purpose? I am living proof. My life has been filled with incredible highs but also heart-wrenching gut punches and losses. Looking back, it is not in the victories that I've learned my lessons; the victories are the times to thank God, exhale, make a mental and soulful note, and marinate in all the goodness of the moment; the win. It's in the lessons, the stumbles, the brutality of loss where I've really been forged; where my character was formed and tested. In the darkest moments is where the true Rachel Joy was formed.

In the fall of 2016, I was a sportscaster flying high. I was the first female host on SiriusXM college channels. I was also voting for the Heisman and hosting the College Football Playoff. It was a great time professionally, but it was a dark time in college football.

Here is an excerpt from an article I wrote that season. Little did I know it would spark something in me, in the deepest part of my soul, that at the same time it would heal me . . . to my core, and it would help me start a literal movement that would change and save countless lives. You do not know the power of your pain until you harness it, process it, and use it constructively to help others.

College football is breaking my heart.

I literally broke down and cried during a break Wednesday on Sirius XM College Sports Nation.

Everywhere I turn these days, there is news of horrid sexual allegations, rape, blame-shifting, cheating (level 1 and 2), gross misappropriation of funds, illegal gun-toting, plausible deniability, and general lawlessness by players and coaches. Entitlement and enabling runs rampant. What is born early in a player's career, oftentimes, is fostered by a coach's "savior complex."

It is not a good time for college football, and that is an understatement.

I sat in a grocery store parking lot and read Tony Barnhart's initial tweet on the story of the abuse. My first feeling was numbness, shock. Then something started to burn in the pit of my stomach. I was angry and sad, all at the same time.

It brought up a memory I had pushed far down deep, one I had not even shared with my own family until today. But it came barreling back like a searing-hot poker in my gut.

You see, I was once a victim (now I am a victor). Late one night, I was in a familiar house with a familiar somebody, and he was uncharacteristically angry. He dragged me from one end of the house to the other by my hair. There were other people in the house, supposedly sleeping. I screamed for help, but no one came to my aid. Finally, he relented. I curled up into a ball and went to sleep. The next day, I had chunks of hair missing from my head, and carpet burns covered my body. But what hurt worse than my injuries was the fact that people heard my (bloody-murder) screams, yet they refused to help me.

Why? When I go back to that night, that's the resounding question I have. "How could you?"

That's why I can identify with these victims at campuses across the country. I am one of them. And they are me, and a great deal of us was ignored in our most vulnerable hour.

So, I will leave you with this: what are we going to do to take our game back? Where are our leaders? Our makers of men? Where are the responsible fans, you know, the ones that think for themselves, rather than blindly follow their school's every decision?

Where are the teammates strong enough to tell another when they are wrong? Where are the coaches that are willing to say, "Sometimes doing the right thing might cost me something, but I'm willing to do it!"

It's high time for these people to stand up and take the game back that we love.

Who's with me?

Soon after this piece was published, it went viral. But before I sent it to my editor, I remember calling my parents and telling them, "Hey, this happened. I was too ashamed to tell you at the time (because many victims are), but it's going to be published. I'm going to talk about being a victim, but now a victor. I'm going to use my pain for a purpose." I remember my dearly departed momma crying for me, asking me if I was sure. They were heartbroken that I had never shared the details of that horrific night. I told her, "Yes. I've never been more sure of anything in my life." And with those words, the entire trajectory of my life changed with an act of radical vulnerability.

Not long after the article came out, I was invited to speak at the FSU football program. In December of 2016, I spoke to Clemson football fourteen days before they won a national championship. Rather than talk about athletics, I spoke about legacy, trending for something positive, climbing Kilimanjaro for my friend with ALS, and the night I was drug from one end of the house to the other by my hair.

Do I wish this had never happened to me? Of course, but we aren't promised a life free from pain or strife. It is this particular pain that now allows me to say, "I've been there too. I get it. I understand." And while I wish I were never a victim, it is in these bonding moments that I am healed.

I am often asked if my talks are well received, do they listen and absorb? The answer is yes, so much yes, for some. Because here's the reality, you nor I will ever affect them all, but if you can just change one, then you have won. They line up, wait to talk to me, pour out their hearts, cry, keep in touch, and are radically vulnerable too.

I feel like I blinked, and here I am five years later. Since that fateful decision to be brave, I created an actual movement called #ImChangingtheNarrative. I have now spoken to over fifty colleges (to both kings/queens separately). I train and coach others to create movements and become public speakers. I work with Customs and Border Patrol, law enforcement in multiple states, prison ministry, high schools, companies, churches, have a successful live mastermind, a free e-book, an upcoming book in 2023, and I am a part of this amazing project. I still speak on everything I did before but now have a heavy focus on mental health; this is all because I chose to take off my mask and use my pain for a purpose.

As you read a snippet of my story, what memory comes to mind? Is there a pain point?

Keep this in mind: oftentimes, our greatest pain is attached to our greatest purpose.

Sit with that.

And what pains you will be entirely different than what pains me. Another way of inspecting your soul is to figure out what bothers you, deep down? It might be a news story you read or see that you can't shake? What can you do to solve that? **You can change the narrative. You can change the world.**

Trust me on this. I have watched it happen in my life, so much so that I walked away from sportscasting in 2019 after hosting our first mental health game between the University of Maryland and Minnesota football teams. I knew in my soul that I was meant to foster, lead, and teach with #ImChangingtheNarrative, full-time. Sportscasting no longer set my soul on fire. I know everything that came before 2016 was simply a lead-up to what I do now.

Do not curse your struggle. If you sit with it, I promise you there is transformation there.

Trust me on this.

But you have to be brave enough to hold your pain (whether it's traumatic or not traumatic), examine it, forgive people (even the ones that haven't asked), seek therapy, and do the work. Do whatever it takes to get on the other side of bitterness to find the promised land beyond anger. And maybe you've done the work already. BRAVO! Now it's time to take off your mask and share so you can help others. There is someone on your path that desperately needs to hear your story. There is someone that needs to know how you overcame it. Their life may depend on it.

I believe in you.
I see you.
Your story matters greatly.
I am holding space for you.
~Rachel Joy Baribeau

ABOUT THE AUTHOR:

Social Media:
IG @rachelbaribeau
FB @rachelbaribeau
Email rachel@rachelbaribeau.com

In 2016, ground-breaking national sportscaster Rachel Joy Baribeau penned a piece for GridironNow entitled, *"College Football is Breaking My Heart."* The game she loved was becoming unrecognizable. Negative news stories dominated the game, and no campus seemed immune. Most broadcasters would have left it at that.

Not Rachel.

Rachel developed #ImChangingtheNarrative with student-athletes in mind and a belief that one crooked course made straight is everything. One misstep not taken means one less victim in the world. And one less life is thrown away because of a split-second bad decision.

At Rachel's first visit, sometimes they're skeptical when the petite Latina woman is introduced, but in just sixty minutes, she wins them over. She now speaks to athletes, law enforcement, churches, corporations, halfway houses, high schools, and more about taking back the headlines for good showing them that they have the power to change the narrative and to find their purpose in life outside of their sport and everyday lives.

To live lives of . . . .

Purpose, Passion, and Platform.

Just like her inspiration, Alabama and NFL star Kevin Turner did before he succumbed to ALS and CTE.

When she's finished, they wait in line to speak to her. They tweet, private message, and text her. They trust her and report back on their efforts to become the kings and queens she consistently challenges them. While the message originated as purpose, passion, platform, over five-plus years and fifty campuses, it now encompasses, heavily, mental health, being a king/queen every day of your life, and interpersonal relationships, as Rachel was a victim of domestic violence herself.

When she's not scaling the world's tallest freestanding mountain to raise money for ALS or speaking from a stage or computer near you, she enjoys working one-on-one to help others find their own personal #ImChangingtheNarrative and reclaim their God-given JOY!

DON'T VOTE YOURSELF OFF THE ISLAND
Sharon Hughes

All too often, people think if they are not experiencing fandom on social media, giving a Ted Talk, or having a huge platform, somehow, they are irrelevant. These folks disqualify themselves from influencing the world around them. Does this resonate with you? If so, you are in the right place. We have some work to do together to uncover how and where you will use your influence, and I will share with you the surprising way I found mine.

To start, let's take a step back—what do you want to say to the world? Maybe you're not sure, and that is okay. However, you will have an outline and begin reframing your experiences so they can be turned into your message to influence others by the time we are done.

Do you think your past mistakes make your message less relevant? If so, I beg to differ. No matter what you have done or has happened to you, you have what it takes to succeed and an answer to someone else's problem.

Are you wondering how I can be so sure? I hope so because that is what I am about to share with you. My hope is as we work together, you will realize what you perceive as "a sea of unworthiness and mistakes" is what shaped your character for this time in your life. Those things you want to keep hidden away, the "hot mess" part of you—is a valuable hidden treasure. I'm guessing no one sent you the memo; it's okay they didn't send it to me either.

Everything you have done, walked through, crawled through, cried through, or are in the middle of now, has and is preparing you for such a time as this very moment. So, now that we have that out of the way, let's get started.

Finding Your Treasure

Start by taking a few seconds right now to think back over all the things you have been through and have overcome.

I'll wait.

Ready? What came to mind for you? Did you wonder how you made it through the tough times when money was tight or family and friends were not there? When everything fell apart, and you were completely lost? Did you take a deep breath of gratitude that it is over, and you are still standing?

Stop here. Do not miss the point. YOU ARE STILL STANDING. I know because if you were not, you would not be reading this book, am I right?

Now, begin thinking of all the things you have learned about yourself, how you have grown as a person, your work ethic, guiding principles, and the sacrifices you made to get where you are. Maybe you worked multiple jobs to make ends meet, lost all your possessions, overcame addiction, or even buried a loved one.

Are you starting to disqualify yourself as if those things were suddenly not that big of a deal and certainly, not worthy of influence?

Don't. These are your treasures, your gifts to the world. You, my friend, are the hero of your story. The story someone needs to hear; you just have not realized it yet.

Your assignment is to begin a running list of all the things I told you to think about above–the things you have learned about yourself and overcome, your guiding principles, all the sacrifices that helped you survive the tough times. Keep adding to your list over the next few days.

As you review the list, what is the overarching theme? What patterns do you see emerging from your list? It is okay if you need to sit with it for a few days to make sense of it; this is the "fleshing out" part. We'll come back to this later.

How I Found My Treasure

I grew up with tremendous dysfunction. No, not "the kind of function that is full of fun"–more like "crazy train, somebody needs to go to jail" dysfunction. And I hid from my story for decades. I was ashamed, embarrassed, and afraid of what people would think of me if they knew the truth. I thought I was unworthy of success, love, the big break, and all the things I had wished for even though I had been successful in many areas of my life.

When I look back at my list of what I overcame, it reads like this: abused by the ones who should have protected me, parental abduction, being drugged and waking up in a garage, abandonment, homelessness, a high school dropout, and a divorcee. But these are not the definition of who I am.

My highlight reel reads like this: a cover model, a fitness trainer, owner of an international home décor line, host of entrepreneurial events, award-winning author, and podcaster. Which of these do you think I learned the most from overall? Would it surprise you to know both, but in completely unusual ways?

Both lists contributed to who I am and prepared me to be the hero of my story, which I didn't know until just a few years ago. Want to know what the game-changing question was? I thought you would never ask! It very well may be the key you are looking for too.

One morning I was lying in bed praying, and I said to God, "I'm not going to make it through this." I heard him say, "What are you believing about yourself?" I thought, "You know all the things. I have a list." And then He said, "Is it true?"

No one had ever asked me if what I believed about myself was true before that moment. My world was completely and forever changed. That question became the foundation of my first book, *The*

Girl in The Garage: Three Steps to Letting Go of Your Past, and the coaching and speaking work I do.

Using My Treasure

Right after that life-changing conversation with the Lord God Almighty, I went into corporate training. I had the opportunity to create any type of training the company could benefit from or want. I was elated, to say the least, but I had my work cut out for me. One hurdle to effective influencing is trust. If your audience does not trust you, it will not matter if you can walk on water like Jesus himself; they will not act on the information.

The first step was meeting with each department manager, asking what they needed, and getting buy-in. To my surprise, they all wanted soft skills training for their teams unanimously. From my life-coaching experience, I knew people respond to the world around them based on their worldview, which also affects how they see themselves, which in turn affects how they act. At the same time, Human Resources was having a retention problem and wanted training that would help shape the company's culture; this was an exciting challenge, and I knew I could make a difference.

I felt completely blessed that I had an opportunity to influence people in the workplace and truly make a difference that could change not just the company but the very lives of the people that worked there. After spending countless hours creating the training that I believed would shift people to think for themselves and not against themselves, the day to present the training had come.

I had a mixed room, with people from different departments, genders, ages, and ethnicities; this was the perfect testing ground to pose God's question, and I was excited!

I opened with a simple question: "What is the thing you've been dragging around your whole life that you can't get over?" I instructed them not to share it and keep it to themselves. Some looked surprised; others looked perplexed. I elaborated, "It could be the coach that said you were not good enough to make the cut, the spouse that walked out on you, or even the parent or teacher who said you were stupid, and you needed to try harder."

Forty-five minutes later, at the end of the training session, I circled back to the opening question and framed it like this: "What is the thing you have been dragging around your whole life that you cannot get over? What if it is not true? Who or what would you be?" The room was silent except for one lady sitting in the front row who blurted out, "Free! I'd be free!"

I knew I was onto something big here. This question, God's question, changed everything. A few hours later, the woman from the front row approached me and shared how eye-opening the training was for her and how that one question would change how she parented. I was elated and found myself blinking back tears of joy. The power to influence was so real and so easy to do.

A few weeks later, I delivered the training to another diverse group and was shocked at the response. Again, at the end of the training, I asked the same questions: "What is the thing you have been dragging around your whole life that you cannot get over? What if it is not true? Who or what would you be?" Two people began to cry! One of the people that started to cry was a man in his mid-thirties. After the training session, he told me he had not spoken to his family in nearly ten years and would be calling them that night. I marveled at the fact that "the question" did not have to be asked during a prayer, as in my case, but could be asked in a corporate training session, and that blew my mind!

The question has the potential to rewrite the story of not only what people believe about themselves but what they believe about their relationships. I have incorporated it into everything I do, whether speaking, coaching, or in interviews, and the results are just as profound every time.

Refining Your Treasure

Going back to the running list, I told you to start writing earlier, and considering all you have learned about yourself and overcome, what made you pivot in your past? If you have not pivoted yet, that is okay–you will get there. As we continue sifting the sand out of the way, you will discover your treasure. It's probably staring you straight in the face right now, but you are too close to it to notice. Be careful not to dismiss your treasure because you think it is "not a big deal."

I want to let you in on a secret, keep this in your pocket for whatever it is worth. Not everyone will resonate with your treasure, and that is okay. If I posed my big "God question" to one hundred people, how many do you think would answer it honestly? How many would allow the answer to change themself? You might be surprised to know many people will not, simply because it is so confrontational and requires changing.

The topic goes deep down the psychology rabbit hole but believe it or not, some people identify so strongly with *who they think they are* that they cannot fathom being free like the lady in the front row wanted to be. Crazy, right?

When you uncover your treasure, it will help the people who are ready to receive it when they are ready. You see, that is two completely different matters altogether, and it is really that simple. It will drive you absolutely bananas knowing you hold the key to their problem, and they are not ready to unlock the door. You will know full well that you could save them so much frustration and even heartache if they would simply listen to what you want to share, but they won't because of where they are on their personal journey of growth.

Going back to your list, what did you overcome that would have gone smoother, faster, or even could have been avoided if you had a mentor? Or a "what to do if this happens" book? How you just answered are clues to your treasure.

To help you refine who you want to influence, consider these questions:

Who are you passionate about? The homeless? Veterans? At-risk youth? Students? Your team at the office? Struggling entrepreneurs?

What issues are you deeply concerned about most?

Do you want to volunteer for a nonprofit, do you want to be paid for your expertise, or both?

Do you want to help others in person, via videos, books, or podcasts (nowadays, you are not limited and can do all of these and reach more people)?

Take notice of the issues and people you are concerned about aligning with any of your experiences and what you have overcome.

Are you still wondering what your hidden treasure is? I will not have done my job here if I did not ask you what you believe about yourself and if it is true. Who would you be, and how would you act if you let go of the things you have believed about yourself that are not true?

Plant Your Flag on The Island

By now, you should have a fairly good idea of what your treasure is and how you will use it to influence the world around you. Next is what I call the easy-hard part; it is the preparation time. The timeline is different for everyone but still part of the process.

There were pieces of my treasure leaving hints for decades, but I was stuck in unworthiness-land and could not see it. There were even times I had significant breakthroughs, but until the day I hit rock bottom and told God I was not going to make it, I was not ready. Whether it works this way for you, I cannot say, but surrender to the process is definitely needed, along with a dose of patience.

Spend time getting clear on what you have to say to the world while staying one hundred percent true to yourself and guiding principles (A.K.A. values). Resist any temptation to take shortcuts or compromise what you stand for. People can smell it a mile away, and it will break the trust factor that you have to have to be a successful influencer.

I want to congratulate you for making it this far, for not giving up and turning the page. What you have to say is important, valuable, and needed. People are searching for the answers that are within them. If you do not move forward, you are withholding a blessing that could change the trajectory of someone's life, as well as yours. That's heavy.

You have your treasure, and it's time to plant your flag on the island of influence. Go ahead, stake your claim. I want to be the first to welcome you to the club. I can't wait to see what you do next!

ABOUT THE AUTHOR:

Social Media:

IG @sharonhughesofficial

FB @calledtoconfidence

Email sharon@sharonhughes.net

Sharon Hughes – Confidence and Self-worth Expert, Author, Speaker, Coach

Sharon is the award-winning author of the best-selling book, *The Girl in The Garage: 3 Steps to Letting Go of Your Past.* She has helped women from all walks of life gain confidence and healthy self-worth to raise their hand in the boardroom, break up with people-pleasing, make peace with their bodies, and let go of the lies they believe about themselves that holds them back from being who God created them to be.

Sharon is famous for pointing out "believing a lie is just as powerful as believing the truth." In her book, she shares how she not-so-bravely stepped into the truth of who she is and triumphed over the unthinkable from parental abduction, homelessness, and even waking up in a garage after being drugged.

In addition, Sharon owes her success to her faith in God, knowing that He prepared her for such a time as this. She offers several courses, including Confidence Academy.

When she's not coaching women, recording her podcast, or plotting her next book, you can find Sharon gazing at a California sunset, petting every dog that crosses her path, and eating obscene amounts of popcorn.

Recipient of Reader's Favorite Silver Medal – Christian Biblical Counseling

For information on the courses Sharon offers, please visit sharonhughes.net/offerings

To book an interview or invite her to speak, please email hello@sharonhughes.net

TWIN IMPACT
Tami Matheny

In October of 1969, an excited young, expecting mother's dreams were crushed when she miscarried. Things turned for the worst when the doctors said she needed to have a complete hysterectomy in April of 1970. All this young lady had ever wanted was to be a mother, and her biggest dream in life was now gone.

She awoke from the hysterectomy with grief and sadness. The first thing she saw was her husband standing over her with excitement in his eyes. "Honey, we are pregnant!" he said, full of enthusiasm. This young woman thought her husband was playing a cruel joke on her. How could he be joking about that at a moment like this? Only when the doctor came in and confirmed it did she realize a miracle had happened. At the beginning of the surgery, the doctor had found she was pregnant, and he did not complete the full hysterectomy.

How could this be? After the miscarriage in October, she was told she wouldn't be able to have children. Now she was pregnant? This didn't add up in the young lady's mind. Technology was nowhere near as advanced as it is now, so the doctors couldn't determine how far along she was.

During a doctor's visit in July, she received greater news. She was pregnant not with one, but with at least two babies. The doctor could feel more than four limbs, but only one heartbeat. They later determined that the hearts were positioned on top of each other, so the doctor could only feel one heartbeat. In October of 1970, a full year after losing her first pregnancy, doctors confirmed with imaging that this mother and her husband would be parents to twins!

This young woman had gone through a heartbreaking event, only to realize that she was being doubly blessed. She had always dreamed of having twins, as far back as she could remember. She had grown up near an aunt with twins and had thought it was so cool. Her favorite television show had twins. Often, while watching the show, she would cry because she wanted twins so badly.

As much as she loved being pregnant, and even though she felt blessed, October through December was trying. Again, the doctors had not been able to determine when she got pregnant, so they could only guess at the due date. For over two long months, she had nightly contractions, only to realize time and time again that it was false labor. Then, early in the morning on December 3, 1970, she gave birth to what she called her "miracle babies."

I happened to be one of those twins, or one of my mom's miracles, as she says. I recall the impact this story had on me as a young child. I loved to hear my mom tell this story over and over. When I look back, I have no doubt it made a huge impact on my belief system. I couldn't realize or explain it at that age, but I do remember my brain always coming back to this story and believing that anything was possible. If my mom could wake up from surgery to prevent her from bearing children to find she was pregnant with twins, then there was hope in every situation. This "miracle event" was the foundation for the outlook I've generally had most of my life.

During our time in the womb, I do not doubt that the personalities of myself and my brother, David, took shape. It's hard to describe, but after spending nine months in a womb together, we developed a bond that no one can explain.

I was the first one to make an appearance. My parents like to say I was eager to get out in the world and see what was there. David took another thirteen minutes, which I'm sure seemed like an eternity to my mom, before showing himself. My family likes to joke and say David was a gentleman for letting me go first. I liked to tease him and say he was scared and pushed me out to see if it was going to be all right in the world.

My parents had known other twins that hated each other. They had a fear that their twins would hate each other, so from day one, they were very intentional about making sure that didn't happen. We had our own rooms, but I wanted to sleep in Dave's room. In my mind, I needed to be by his side, always. When it was time to start school, the principal and teachers said we needed to be in different classrooms. My parents wouldn't hear of it. However, they did tell us we had to make other friends, or they would separate us. I never shared it with anyone, but the thought of being separated from David terrified me, so it forced me to make friends. We were in the same class until sixth grade.

From the beginning, I had a built-in companion and friend. At an early age, we even had the same imaginary friend. We instinctively knew what Bob was doing, at the amazement of my family, or in my grandmothers' case, concern.

One weekend, my parents were out of town, and they had taken us to stay with our grandparents. They had forgotten to tell my Maw Maw about "Bob." As she was making breakfast, she came to sit down at the table with us. Simultaneously, we both screamed, "Don't sit on Bob!" When my parents returned, she met them at the door and said, "I think there is something wrong with the twins." My parents tried to explain, but I'm not sure her fears were ever alleviated.

My grandmother was more at ease when our parents explained that Bob couldn't start school with us. The day before our first day of school, we woke up, and without ever talking about it, we told our family that Bob was getting married and would be moving away. That was the end of Bob.

During Easter, before we were to start Kindergarten, we went on a family trip to Disney World. It was anything but magical. Part of me (David) got deathly sick. For a while, I thought David was part of me. In my mind, we were two halves of a whole.

David had recently gotten over a bad case of measles, but the doctor said he was fine to make the trip. By the time we got to our hotel, he was anything but fine. He was extremely sick. We didn't even check into the hotel. An ambulance was called to the hotel, and before I knew it, David was rushed to the hospital.

I was confused and scared. My parents were too, especially when the doctor told them bluntly that if he made it through the night, he would live. Fortunately, I didn't know that, but I can only imagine the emotions my parents felt. He survived the night. However, the doctors said he had hepatitis and would need to stay in the hospital in Florida for a while.

The next thing I knew, dad and I were returning home to North Carolina without my mom or my Dave. On the way home, I remember asking, "Dad, is Dave going to die?"

I vividly recall him gently patting me, smiling, and saying, "He is going to be okay." I don't think I was fearful that anything else besides Dave coming home healthy was possible. I knew inside it was going to be all right. I would tell others that as well.

One such time stands out. One of our grandmothers was a worrier. When she was taking care of me, I could sense her angst. I asked her what was wrong, and after she told me she was worried about David, I calmly let her know that Dave was going to be okay. I must have been sure of this because it instantly changed her mood.

David was in the hospital for over three weeks. This seemed much longer for me, and I felt like more than half of me was missing. Not only was Dave not with me, but my mom and my other grandmother had flown to Florida to be with him. Still, for what a five-year-old could comprehend, I knew it would be okay.

As we grew up, we became like night and day. He wasn't very talkative. If I knew you, you couldn't get me to shut up. I was opinionated and liked to get my way. David was mild and kind. I had to win. He was a good sport. As we got older, we both excelled in the classroom and were good athletes. I often struggled with comparisons between myself and David. Even so, I never blamed him or became jealous of him.

David was the same. I received more recognition in sports than he did. I know it had to eat him up when people at school would rag him about his sister being a better athlete than him, but he never let that affect how he treated me. He was always my biggest fan.

In my senior year, my high school basketball team was playing our arch-rival that we hadn't beaten in over five years. We were down one with just seconds left, and I was fouled. I had to make both foul shots, and we would win one of the biggest games in the program's history. Miss them, and my legacy was gone. A timeout was called, and I had time to think of these things. My heart was pounding harder than I had ever felt, and my hands were sweaty. I wasn't sure my legs could carry me to the foul line. Then, I happened to scan the crowd. I saw David and I knew from his look that I could and would make both shots, and I did.

I've heard people complain about being a twin, and many don't have fond memories of growing up that way. Maybe I'm lucky, or maybe it truly is a miracle. But being a twin has been the single most important and impactful thing in my life. I wouldn't trade it for the world. It has shaped and created the me that I am.

No matter how dark something seems, and when it seems like no one else is there, I know David is.

The impact of being a twin and the circumstances of my birth created the power of belief and positivity in me that has helped me be successful and happy. Growing up with the twin that God blessed me with helped me develop creativity and learn how to play and work with others. When you are a twin, you learn early on that it's not just about you (yes, I've battled that at times, especially when I was younger).

If you know me, then you know how "This is Good" is my life's motto. The saying comes from an African Folktale that I share below. This story has influenced me personally and professionally.

There was an African king who had a best friend whom he kept close to him. The friend had a habit of looking at every situation that occurred in his life as positive and he would often say, "This is good!" Because of this, the king took his friend with him wherever he went. One day the king and his friend were out on a hunting expedition. The friend loaded the rifle for the king and when the king fired it, it backfired and blew off his thumb. The friend as usual said, "This is good!" to which the king replied, "No, this is NOT good!" and angrily sent his friend to jail. All the way to jail, the friend said, "This is good." Once in jail, every day the friend continued to say, "This is good." The other people in jail would reply, "You're crazy. Your best friend threw you in jail. This isn't good." But the friend would smile and again say, "This is good." A year and a half passed, and the friend was still in jail. In the meantime, the king goes on another hunting party, and they are captured by a band of cannibals. The cannibals began to kill and eat the hunting party one by one. However, the cannibals were extremely superstitious and would not kill nor eat anything that wasn't whole. When they got to the king and saw he was missing a thumb, they immediately let him go. The king rushed to the jail where his friend was imprisoned, got on his knees, and said, "Please forgive me. You saved my life! Thank you, thank you." To which his friend replied, "This is good!" "Yes, this is good for me, but I've wasted a year and half of your life. I am so sorry," replied the king. "No," his friend explained, "This is good for me too!" "What do you mean?" asked the king. "How is it good that I sent you to jail for over a year?" "If I had NOT been in jail, I would have been with you and killed by the cannibals." -African folktale

Although the story is a bit dramatic compared to what most of us face daily, this story illustrates the point that regardless of what happens in life, we can choose our perspective. We can prevent ourselves from enduring worse or allow something better to occur. Having a "this is good" mindset doesn't mean you won't have challenges. It means you'll use those challenges to push you to something greater.

My mom's pregnancy, and ultimately our birth, have been the ultimate this-is-good story. The heartbreak that my mom must have felt was replaced with her dream. Even when things look bleak if we keep our faith we allow something different, yet better to transpire.

From our appearance in our mom's womb to our life side by side, being a twin created the power of belief in me that has been the center point of my life.

ABOUT THE AUTHOR:

Social Media:

IG @Refuse2LoseCoaching
Email tamilmatheny@gmail.com

Tami Matheny is the owner of Refuse2LoseCoaching LLC. She is an author, speaker, and member of the Jon Gordon Team. As a mental game coach, she assists people in all walks of life with improved confidence, focus, motivation, mental toughness, leadership, teamwork, and more. Tami has a passion for helping others build a foundation of confidence and overcoming adversity. She has seen first-hand how confidence is key to success in any area in life.

Although she was a standout athlete and student at East Rutherford High School, Tami struggled with maintaining confidence. Confidence continued to elude her during her time at Lenoir-Rhyne College, where she played basketball and tennis while earning a degree in psychology. She went on to receive a master's degree in Sports Administration from the University of North Carolina. It wasn't until she became the men's and women's tennis coach at the University of South Carolina Upstate that she began her journey of exploring and researching confidence. Not only did this lead her to discover how to maintain it for herself, but it led her to where she is today. Today, Tami's goal is to help others on their journey.

When she's not working with others, Tami remains physically active. She has completed a handful of marathons, including the Boston Marathon and ultramarathons. Her longest race to date is a forty-miler. She is an avid cyclist, completing rides over eighty miles. Tami continues to seek new mental and physical challenges.

Tami's books include: "The Confident Athlete," "This is Good: A Journey on Overcoming Adversity," "The Confidence Journal," and "Challenger Deep: Stories, Fables, and Lessons to Help You Rise Above Adversity."

GOING THROUGH THE FIRE
Tamesha Allen

On March 23, 2021, my life changed forever. I had to undergo a surgery called a laparoscopic hysterectomy. I found out in November 2020 that I had several enlarged uterine fibroids. My heart dropped.

I knew I had one fibroid years ago, and the female doctor at the time mentioned that, unless I was in pain, surgery was not necessary. Unfortunately, I allowed the influence of that doctor to make the decision not to pursue the procedure.

That was the biggest mistake I have ever made. During 2020, COVID-19 shook the world, and everyone had to adjust to a new "normal." I became sick in late March 2020 and was not quite sure why. At the time, I worked for a K-8 school, and we decided to switch to e-learning due to the rapid spread of the pandemic. I have worked in the realm of education for twenty years. There were times in my career when I would work in K-12 and higher education simultaneously. Along with my role as an educator, I am also an inspirational speaker, a scholarship strategist, and youth and young adult advocate.

When the pandemic hit, everything shifted. My illness caused a lot of pain and grief for those who surrounded me. My symptoms worsened as time passed. I took matters into my own hands, trying to figure out what was wrong. Fear and anxiety began to sink in, and I felt that my mental health was in jeopardy. One day, I felt like a ton of bricks had fallen on me, and I could not move. I had a headache and chest pain that would not go away. Although I was not sure, I immediately thought it was COVID-19.

Unfortunately, I could not get tested at the time due to the limited supply, so my doctor instructed me to wait it out. Time passed, and my symptoms grew worse. I called my mother the next day, and she stopped by with some aspirin and cod liver oil. I grew up with the life principle of holistic medicine. Although there are medicinal properties to some home remedies, I needed something stronger than what my mom gave me.

The next day, my mother and middle sister stopped by my house with vitamin C. It helped a little, but there was something else attacking my body, and it did not let go. I tried everything—vitamin C, zinc, garlic, cinnamon, honey, lemon, elderberry, and turmeric. These are great, but something else was wrong, and I could not put my finger on it. I was frustrated. I emailed the principal of my school to let him know I wasn't feeling well and needed to schedule a doctor's visit. On April fourth, I scheduled an immediate virtual visit at my doctor's office to receive some insight into my symptoms. After asking me the COVID screening questions, the doctor's nurse relayed the message that it was just stress. She said to wait it out, and if my symptoms worsen, go to the ER immediately. Was stress the best she could come up with for a diagnosis?

That night, I felt worse, and the only person I knew who could help me fight this battle was the one whose name is above all names—Jehovah Rapha, God, my healer! I cried out like never before and asked God to heal me. My symptoms grew worse, and I decided to visit the emergency room. I informed all those close to me, and when I arrived, it was not a pleasant experience. After I checked in and the doctor ordered some simple tests, I was discharged because everything came back normal. Normal? I did not feel normal. I felt like I was going to die. I called a female friend who works as a medical assistant to see if she could shed some light on my situation, and she said the same thing as the others—you have to wait it out.

I had been waiting for too long and was becoming even more frustrated. I continued to advocate for myself to get some real answers. Months had gone by, and with my health concerns, I decided to work from home. I started a remote position working for a college, and it has been a blessing. I could not risk returning to an in-person or hybrid environment, especially while trying to figure out my health crisis.

My emotions were running high, and I became angry. I continued to visit the ER, only for them to tell me my vital signs were good and the tests were normal. I felt abandoned, defeated, and dismissed. I was on my second female doctor at a different health network, and I needed answers. I kept advocating for myself and still did not receive what I needed—help!

While I was enduring this pain, I reached out to a woman who I thought could help me: my father's middle sister, who is also a medical professional. I shared my symptoms with her, and she encouraged me to keep fighting for my health. In fact, she would educate me on the next steps to take. My aunt has worked in the medical profession for over twenty-five years and still does to this day. Now, if she did not know something, she would encourage me to reach out to my primary physician. She was a gift from God!

After all her counsel and advice, I kept trying to find the root cause of my pain. One day, I made an appointment with my new female doctor. I shared my symptoms, and she checked my vitals and did some blood work, along with a physical exam. Within forty-eight hours, I received a phone call from the doctor's office saying they found an infection in my body. I was confused and did not know why. I took an antibiotic for seven days and scheduled a follow-up appointment.

After taking the antibiotic, I called my aunt to update her. I did feel better but not healthy. I still was experiencing pain, and this time, it was abdominal pain. During my follow-up appointment, I still felt like the new doctor was hearing me, but not listening to the symptoms I was experiencing. All she wanted to do was medicate me, and I am not too fond of medicine unless absolutely needed. By the time the visit was over, I was livid. I felt like the invisible Black Woman. I felt hopeless and helpless. I no longer shared my symptoms with anyone. I had to work through the pain. Every morning when I awoke, I thanked God for another day and asked Him, "Why haven't You healed me yet?"

When I didn't receive the answer I needed, I went on about my day. On September 7, 2021, I asked a few co-workers about switching to a new female doctor for the third time. Two of them recommended one of the best primary care physicians in this particular network. I researched her credibility and found she had a five-star rating, which was perfect! I felt relieved and scheduled an appointment with her immediately.

A couple of days before my appointment, I had time to reflect on all that had happened these past few months. A couple of my so-called female friends at the time betrayed me. They were talking about me behind my back to their other friends and family about my situation. The disturbing thing is that they opened their homes to me. The first one I stayed with was the medical assistant for about two weeks, and I stayed with the other one for one week.

One day, I received a call from the medical assistant to check in, and amid the conversation, she mentioned I needed an anxiety pill. She acted as if I also needed a straitjacket. Now, I am not against anyone who needs medicine for any reason. However, I knew something was not right with my body, and no anxiety pill was going to cure it. After that conversation, I withdrew from everyone. Every time someone inquired about my health, I told them I was fine and left it at that.

About a week or two later, I reconnected with my godsister, Kisha, and I also reached out to my other two friends, Mark and Melissa. They kept me encouraged and motivated while enduring this trial. Every day, I would spend time with God in prayer. One morning, I prayed and asked God to send individuals who could help me, not due to obligation or for their glory, but for His glory. I was also encouraged to enroll in therapy. Although I am a natural extrovert, I was reluctant. I did not want anyone to know my personal business. I am also a private person and don't let people into my space easily.

However, I decided to let God work this out, and I no longer wanted to carry this burden. One day, He answered my prayer. My breakthrough was around the corner! God sent me four powerhouse ladies to get me back on track: Monique Elliott, a licensed counselor, social worker, author, and speaker; Sybil Satterfield, a speaker, life coach, herbalist, and entrepreneur; Lexi Johnson, author, international speaker, entrepreneur, and financial coach; and Yvonne Collins, chief financial officer, speaker, and mentor. The common denominator among these women is that they are all speakers and coaches.

These four powerhouse women brought strength, wisdom, compassion, accountability, and prayer into my life. All of them played an instrumental role in my life, and they still do to this day. A few days later, I met with my third female doctor, and she was wonderful. I found outs she believed in holistic healing. Not only did she listen, she genuinely cared about my concerns and had my best interests at heart. She also reviewed my previous medical history from the other two health networks.

One thing she mentioned while performing a physical exam was that I had an enlarged uterus and some fibroids. I was not aware at the time how serious my health condition was, so she referred me to OB/GYN. Later on, she also referred me to see a urologist, gastroenterologist, and neurologist. I found out that fibroids can cause several other issues such as urinary tract infections, irregular bowel movements, abdominal pain, and back pain. Who knew? I didn't.

Before I made appointments with these specialists, I spoke with my therapist, Monique, to help me process my thoughts about my health issues so that I could heal. During this time, I also met with my Auntie Yvonne, Sybil, and Lexi to help me stay mentally and spiritually grounded. There were moments when I needed an immediate response, and they all were there! I developed a routine. I prayed with Auntie Yvonne every night, attended therapy with Monique weekly, participated in life coaching with Sybil twice a month, and spoke to Lexi every few days. I had a circle of women who believed in my healing and didn't think I was crazy. I always updated them on the progress of my journey, and they provided sound advice that gave me a sense of peace.

The day I saw my OB/GYN, she ordered a vaginal scan and ultrasound to see where exactly the fibroids were. I spoke to my prayer partner, therapist, and life coach the day before my appointment because my anxiety was high. I focused on the problem instead of the solution. I was reminded of one of my favorite scriptures. It reads, "Dear friend, I pray that you may enjoy good health and that all may go well with you, even as your soul is getting along well" (3 John 1:2 [NIV]) wants us to prosper and be in good health!

My OB came in and shared the results of my ultrasound. She confirmed what I had been hearing all along—I had an enlarged uterus due to several enlarged fibroids. She proceeded to say that fibroids are usually noncancerous and are most common in African American women. She told me I would need surgery and provided me with options.

I went home to seek council with God and discuss my options with the four women who have impacted my life tremendously. I also shared the news with my godsister, Kisha, my aunt, my sister, my parents, and a few other friends and family members. After much prayer and guidance, I decided to undergo a laparoscopic hysterectomy. The surgery coordinator called, and we scheduled it for March 23, 2021, at 7:00 a.m. I felt both relief and anxiety.

The day before my surgery, I alerted those who needed to know, including the powerhouse ladies. On the day of my surgery, Kisha was by my side. She made sure I was well taken care of and asked all the right questions. My surgery was to be no longer than four hours, or so we thought. I went in at 7:00 a.m., and when I awoke, I looked up and said, "Thank you, Jesus." I looked over at the clock, and it was 2:30 p.m. It took seven and a half hours for my procedure.

After the anesthesia wore off, I informed everyone that the surgery went well. Kisha was there to greet and comfort me, and she told me what had happened. My uterus was so enlarged that the doctors had to make another incision above my belly button to cut the uterus into pieces and pull it through. During my surgery, she called two of the powerhouse ladies, Monique and Auntie Yvonne, to intercede in prayer on my behalf. The next day, the hospital discharged me, and I spent my recovery time at my godsister's house.

During my recovery, I thought about so many teachable moments throughout my journey. The first one was advocacy. As an advocate for others, I learned to do the same for myself. Speak up even when no one else is speaking on your behalf. The second one was knowing the true definition of the word family. Trust and believe, this word exceeds the bloodline. People come and go all the time. However, God always shows you who is truly loyal and who desires your well-being.

Life has a way of knocking you down. Yet you still have the power to rise again. To this day, I share my testimony by raising awareness about uterine fibroids and encouraging women of all ages, especially African American women, to take care of themselves and schedule their annual examinations. Their life depends on it!

ABOUT THE AUTHOR:

Social Media:

IG @tamesha_speaks

FB @tameshaspeaks

Email tamesha@tameshaspeaks.com

Tamesha Allen is an inspirational speaker, author, youth and young adult advocate, educator, scholarship strategist, and seminar leader. She is the owner and operator of Tamesha Speaks, LLC, where she focuses on youth and young adults, education, and inspiring women. Tamesha is also the Founder of Scholarship101: Access, which assists scholars and families with funding for college. When Tamesha speaks, she shifts mindsets toward greatness. She affirms the lives of her audience and encourages change through topics such as "Stand Up & Step Out," "Beauty is Your Name," "To Speak or Not to Speak," and "Why Leave Money on The Table?"

Tamesha has been a featured guest on "Chip Baker—The Success Chronicles" and was also recently featured in the August 2021 issue of My Sister's Keeper Magazine in support of The Timalechi Nursery School of Embangweni, Malawi (Central Africa). She helped raise funds to provide school supplies for the students and help bring clean running water to the school. She holds a master's degree in Student Development Counseling and Administration, and her motto is, "Live every day with purpose, on purpose."

BEAUTY BEGINS ON THE INSIDE AND SPREADS "ABROAD"

Tory Holloway

I have been in the beauty industry for twenty-five years. I love being impactful by creating an atmosphere for change. It's said that beauty is only skin deep, but I beg to differ. Beauty has to be felt. That's why it lies in the eyes of the beholder. It's a quality of life.

I begin my day expecting beauty before I ever apply concealer, foundation, or blush. I exemplify it first with my actions then I apply my lipstick. I always wanted to be a hairstylist growing up in Kilgore, Texas. I'm a proud Alumni of the class of 1996.

I set out to be a force to reckon with when it comes to the glitz and glam of being a stylist. I can recall admiring the legends that came before me back in the day. It only took one visit to the salon. The smell of luster silk and Pump-It-Up would fill the air as the heat of the pressing comb straightened out my kinky treads. Sharon would curl my hair tight with those smoking marcel irons while the blue magic rolled down my neck. I was sure to be fabulous.

My hair would be all fluffy with those curls pushed up full of bounce and shine. I knew I would one day be one of the greats. I would be riding around in a Cadillac with the white walls. That was my motivation at the time. That was impressive for a twelve-year-old—it was either that or First Lady for me. Being a hairstylist exemplified strength and class. I felt beautiful, not just outwardly, but with a beauty that would guide my path of being beautifully made in the image of God my creator.

"Deck thyself now with majesty and excellency, and array thyself with glory and beauty" (Job 40:10 [KJV]).

I never believed that the little girl who dreamed of doing hair would grace the stage with such a talented and successful group of stylists. After many years of doing hair in my hometown, my talent had made room for me and brought me before great people. Moving to the city was definitely a leap of faith for me. It took me thirty-five years to drive to the city of Dallas by myself, but once I conquered that fear, I activated my faith, and I was ready for the lights, camera, action! I wanted to take my skills to the next level. It was show time!

When it came to speaking, I was pretty shy, but performing on stage wasn't as challenging because I loved competition. I won a few and lost a few, but not placing at all pushed me to pursue the work behind the stage, encouraging others to push past their fears. Now that felt like a true calling, for I loved people. Working center stage at the largest Hair Shows in Texas gave me the ability to open the door for others to display their talents on a major platform.

Your biggest competition is yourself. You have to push past your fear, be your greatest self, and accomplish what you set out to do. We were all born to succeed. Even though I love the beauty industry, I felt a longing for a deeper call. I was ready to return to my first love. I realize that the stage was just the beginning of my passion for ministry. I needed more of Him, and it was clear that fear no longer controlled me. I opened the door and allowed Him to guide my every footstep. I was ready to share the love and joy God had given me with others. It was time for Kingdom building.

I always knew I had a passion for working with women, other than just making them look good on the outside. I want to enlighten that glow on the inside. That passion caused me to step out on faith and start a group on Facebook called Lady (loving and doing you).

Out of that group, I developed relationships with some powerful, anointed sisters ready and willing to put their hands to the plow. I was the visionary of the lady conference, born out of the tragedy of 2020, the year the world changed forever. We were in a pandemic, but we pushed through. Despite being married, divorced, single, separated, or widowed, we started a movement of change, linking a group of believers together to ignite a fire within us. It was the beginning of something great. I was impacted by W.O.G (woman of God) which changed my heart. I wanted more of God's power.

The next conference would be called "A Mother's Love", as we all know there is no love like a mother's love. The movement of God fell down in that place and a sisterhood was formed with a chain that would link us together, once and for all. There was power in unity. We were on the move. It was time to boss up because of salvation. The "Boss" conference helped us to identify the opticals we face being a light in the workplace. The challenges we face when we live out our salvation at work may put us in positions that test our faith. Even so, we must focus on our purpose and calling that keeps us grounded in Christ our savior. We must be an example for Him, even at work.

A couple of months after the "Boss" conference, my heart was broken into a thousand pieces due to the loss of my dear cousin. What would I do now that my faith was being tested? I struggled because this one hit too close to home. The Lord had to help me with this one now; a link in the chain was missing. She would always have a song of praise or encouraging words when I needed it.

Even though I wanted to give up, I pushed through the pain, because God had given me the name of the next conferenced the night before she passed— "No Shades of Grey." The theme was this: unapologetically for God I live, and for God, I'll die, period. That service was dedicated to her memory.

We can no longer compromise who we are in Christ. There is no in-between either. You are for Him or against Him. No more straddling the fence. Choose this day who you're going to serve, because no man knows the day or hour that the son of God will return for us.

She will forever live in my heart as a true angel and inspiration. Many powerful women have influenced me to be the W.O.G I am today. I will continue to pour what God has given me into them by creating an atmosphere of change.

I'm a Life Coach, Hairstylist, and Visionary of Lady (loving and doing you). I'm honored to share my testimony that because He lives, I can face tomorrow.

"Then spake Jesus again unto them saying I am the light of the world. He that followeth me shall not walk in darkness, but shall have light of life" (John 8:12 [KJV]).

ABOUT THE AUTHOR:

Social Media:

IG @_truediva_

FB @toryharris-holloway

Email toryharris35@gmail.com

Tory Holloway is the proud owner of Beauty Bar LLC in Mesquite Texas. She has been a licensed cosmetologist for twenty-five years and loves to make her clients feel beautiful from the inside out.

Tory Holloway is also a certified Life Coach and the visionary of Lady (loving and doing you), where she serves as a leader for impacting women to support each other on their spiritual walk with Christ. She has been married to her husband Jason Holloway for eleven years, and she is a proud parent of Shyla Cobb, Timothy Cobb, and two bonus sons, Adonijah Holloway and Bryce Holloway. Tory sets out to create an atmosphere of change by helping others accomplish their dreams and become who they were created to be by emphasizing kingdom building and living on purpose with a purpose.

COFFEE AND LIFE
Vallye Adams

Write a book chapter about someone or something that has **"INFLUENCED"** you, they say? Someone or something that has made an **"Impact"**, a difference in your life, they say…

So, my question is, how do you narrow down almost half of a century to one person (or even a few?) or something that has made an impact on and influenced your life??

Seriously, I know there is about a 99.9% chance you have no idea who I am, so let's introduce ourselves. I'd like to start with, hello, my name is Vallye Adams…yes, odd I know. No, Vallye is not short for anything, it's not "Valerie." It's like "valley" (like hills or mountains) but spelled "Vallye." It's a family name and I'm the 4th Vallye in my family and my oldest daughter's first name is also Vallye so, yes, she's the 5th!! So now you know something about me, and I know nothing about you. Let's change that! Let me start with a challenge. Since you are reading this chapter, I challenge you to go right now to your computer or cell phone and email me, Vallye Adams, at <u>vallye@etavelesolutions.com</u> …share with me, "ONE", only ONE person or ONE something you feel has been the sole influence on you and made an impact and difference in your life and why. If you send me this email and can convince me that you truly have only ONE someone or something, I will promptly email you back a $10 Starbucks gift certificate!! Yes, you read that right! I will be SO happy to receive an email and get to know you…another fun fact: I truly am a strong extrovert and love meeting new people, so I will happily send you a gift if you email me and can convince me of your only ONE influence and or impact from "someone" or "something". Sound good? I am awaiting your email and hear all about your influence or impact person or thing…go for it!!

So perhaps you are wondering, why would this stranger, who knows nothing about me, send me a "Starbucks" gift certificate, just for sending her an email? Let's get the "legal" stuff out of the way: Do I work for Starbucks or get paid in any way to promote them? NO, not at all! Here's another fun fact about me, I LOVE all coffee, everything about coffee and I do love Starbucks! So, now you know my name is a fun fact about me so in essence, now, we are no longer complete strangers. Check!

So, "write a book chapter about one person or something that has impacted and influenced your life…"

Well, you know I love coffee, so I guess I could write an entire book chapter about how coffee has made a profound impact on my life. It has!! It does influence me each and every day. An influence every day…that's impressive! Coffee does impact me as I wake up each morning, barely conscious of the world around me. The thought of the smell, the warmth, the robust chocolaty and nutty flavor, coffee for sure influences me to get out of bed, stumble down the stairs, head to the kitchen, grind those fresh beans and brew a fresh cup of steamy hot coffee!! But you see, coffee, as much of a daily impact and strong influence it has on my life, is only ONE of the hundreds (maybe thousands) of "somethings" that have influenced and impacted me in my lifetime. So why would I write an entire chapter about one thing? Do I think it would be impactful to you, or possibly help make a direct impact on your life if I wrote an entire book chapter on the influence of coffee? Very doubtful…however, feel free to take me up on a very impactful and possibly influential cup or two of coffee by receiving a $10 Starbucks gift card out of this. What do you have to lose??

So, as you might have guessed, I decided not to write about how one specific person influenced me. If you have begun reading other chapters from the extremely successful and influential authors in this book collaboration, entitled "Impact of Influence", Volume 3", they are sharing their version of something or someone who has influenced or impacted their life directly. Well, my chapter will not showcase one specific person or an amazing job or product that impacted my life significantly. It will not draw you into a sentimental, heartfelt, and teary-eyed autobiographical story of my perfect family or one incredible family member who made me who I am today, looking like a scene from "Little Woman" (although trust me, I love me a teary-eyed, family moment from Little Woman scene and analogy any day!!). What this chapter will focus on is what I have learned from the influences of MANY people, from MANY influences, and the MANY impacts gained living and experiencing my entire LIFE. My hope is you will finish the remainder of this chapter, curled up in your favorite cozy, quiet spot, wrapped in the softest blanket, and enjoy a delicious hot cup of coffee or tea (from Starbucks after you emailed me). I hope that you will find something impactful from hearing my influences and impacts are not from "Something or someone" rather "Everything and Everyone!

This chapter will share with you some examples, "take-aways" I have gained from forty-seven years of life (yes, now you know my age and I have dated myself) have made me who I am today. Not one, but countless family members, including my mom, husband (of almost twenty-five years), my three beautiful children, and even my crazy Uncle Al, all have made an incredible and profound impact on me. ALL of my jobs, from my first job at fourteen years old in the local yogurt shop, to property management, real estate, various nonprofits, including my current, self-started, national, nonprofit consulting firm, has and continues to profoundly impact and influence my decisions, beliefs, outcomes, and actions.

Everything I have accomplished, or not, up until this part of my life, has impacted my life. Time, successes, struggles, wins, losses, the best of the best and the lowest of the low: everything and everyone has impacted and shaped who I am, what I have accomplished, and where I am going. In fact, you reading this chapter and me writing this chapter could absolutely impact or influence you and will definitely impact me. Maybe, it will influence us in a way we least expect. However, the possibility is there, this is an opportunity to influence the future for you, for me, for my family, your family, my business, and yours as well. What you and I do every day, ALL of our experiences, and ALL of the people who are in any way, a part of our lives, can and will impact and influence us in everything we do. Perhaps you are fully aware of this statement but I believe strongly that It's HOW we choose to allow these people and experiences to impact and influence us that truly counts. That is how we are impacted and influenced.

But don't worry!! There is no way I possibly have the time or the book space to share with you ALL of the experiences, hundreds of people, and things that have impacted and influenced my life? One cup of coffee would certainly NOT be enough! So let's summarize!! Do you like "acronyms"?

Perhaps you are reading this book because you know one of the many incredibly powerful, driven, and successful female authors. What an honor to be asked and even considered to be a part of this book!! Perhaps you are reading this to gain valuable insight or helpful "take-aways" on influential impact. Maybe you love reading self-help books to learn and focus on tips or ways to make YOU even better than you already are. Friendly reminder: YOU are ENOUGH!! So, what I would like to share with you, (besides a great cup of coffee or tea) is a few of what we'll call, "Vallye's Valuable Visions from L I F E." I thought, let me share with you the most important and valuable "visions" I and use in value from my LIFE's influences that could impact and influence you!

I work well with acronyms. Some people love them, and others truly hate them, with a passion! For me, when they are easy and relate to something I am working on or need to remember, they help me. If you hate them, feel free to jump to the next chapter, enjoy the coffee, and know, I am so happy we are not strangers, but now friends…all good!! In my book, that is always a WIN!

However, if you chose to continue reading, please accept this prewarning and *asterisk* for my LIFE Acronym: statements made most likely and almost certainly will sound "cliché." Again, it's my opinion that it's HOW we use people, things, experiences, and opportunities to influence and impact us. So, if you choose to read on, please do so knowing this could possibly be (no guarantee), your opportunity or your "something" that may have a positive impact or influence you, your family, your job or career or your life, even though it may sound like a cliché. Read this with an open mind. Read and process as a reminder, like a mantra, as a value to your future impact of influence. Again, what do you have to lose??

So, here it goes. My LIFE and valuable lessons learned, visions experienced, impacted, and influenced:

L:

LOOK for positivity
LISTEN with your ears and heart
LEARN every day, from "everyone and everything" you experience.
LOVE what you have and who you LOVE
LIVE every day, time is limited

I:
INCLUDE the forgotten
IGNORE negative people, words, and thoughts
IMPOSSIBLE is NOT an option
INVEST in YOU…. You are enough

F:

FAMILY and "framily"* is everything
FIND and FOCUS on your strengths, not your weaknesses

FOLLOW your passions, heart, and purpose

E:

ENTHUSIASM is contagious…give it and take it
ENVISION your version of success…see it…then believe it to achieve it!!

These "valuable visions" are my mantra. These are what I have learned and have profoundly impacted and influenced my life. These statements are what I remember, say, and focus on when times are tough and need picking up. These statements are what I say and celebrate when times are amazing! Here's a little of my "why."

*LOOK for positivity: One of my top five strengths from the Clifton Strength Finder assessment is "Positivity". (If you want to know the other four, email me!!) Does that mean I am always positive, never see, feel or have negativity? No, absolutely NOT. However, I have been fortunate to have positive people in my life. I try to continually surround myself with positive people. I strive to find people who find, or try to find, positive in every situation, even during negative situations. This is the influence that has impacted my life in so many ways. My goal is to every day, LOOK to find something positive. Positive makes me happy, keeps me moving forward, and looks into the future with joy! Are you more of the "glass is half empty or half full or just happy to have something in the glass," kind of person??

LISTEN with your ears and heart. As an extrovert, type A personality, a public speaker, CEO, and an auctioneer/emcee for nonprofits, I am always talking!! My grandmother (yes, her name was Vallye…Vallye Love) taught me (and I have to remind myself of this often), "sometimes just listen, hear what others are saying, not just with your ears but feel what they are saying with your heart. Listen and you will learn a lot. You don't always have to be heard,

Vallye...listen, with your heart." This has impacted me not only in personal relationships but also in business. This is probably why I am in the nonprofit industry. My heart hears and feels the needs of others, I just need to fully listen to best be able to help and support. When we listen to others, not just with our ears but with our hearts too, we can truly feel and understand them. We then can build the relationship bridge so to fully share, listen and learn. Relationships are the foundation of LIFE, past, present, and future. Definitely a work in progress for me. Are you more of a "Listener" or a "Talker"?

LEARN every day: I believe in the power of learning—every day, from everyone and everything. Some of my most successful and intelligent teachers, colleagues, friends, and bosses influenced this to me. Why? I'm sure they all had their reasons but mine is: If we are learning, we are growing; if we are growing, we are experiencing; if we are experiencing, we are gaining, we will keep moving forward and truly living life to the fullest. Learning does not always have to revolve around the positive. Maybe we learn what we *don't* want to do, how to *not* treat people or how we *don't* want to live...but, we can learn it into the "positive"! Maybe, we learn how to influence or impact ourselves and each other or take something we don't want to do and turn it into a positive. Learning from others is how each of us got to where we are today. My mindset is everyone and everything can teach us something...even those you think have nothing to teach us.... they do! Learn... What do you have to lose? Do you try to learn something new every day??

LOVE what you have and who you love: Sounds pretty simple (and yes, cliché) yet sometimes, most times, it can be so hard to put into action. Wanting more, working more, buying more, more promotions, more money, more vacations, more friends, more clothes, more parties...more, more!! Our society feeds the "more" food and we all eat it! Me included.

Yet the fundamental and most important book in the world teaches us to *"let all that you do be done in LOVE."*

LOVE never gives up…

LOVE never fails…

LOVE above all things…

LOVE others as you love yourself…

I could go on but if we try to remind ourselves daily, to LOVE ourselves because WE are enough, LOVE what and who we have and what and who you want to love, just LOVE. Don't hate. Share love with those who are filled with or spread hate, don't let greed lead, appreciate what we have, find joy and love in being alive… just love. This will impact and influence others in the greatest of ways!

LIVE every day…time is limited: Again, how many times have we heard or said it?? But do we really believe it, live it? My mom got sick in 2003. She died suddenly and very unexpectedly when she was only 53 years old. This loss was devastating, turned my world upside down, and tore apart our entire family. To lose someone so young, so unexpectedly, the matriarch, the glue that keeps everyone and everything together, was profound. I was twenty-eight years old, with two young children and unprepared to face the world without her. For those of you who have lost your mother, or someone close to you, understands this black hole, void, never to be filled. An ache felt daily and to the core. Life and death; loss, a part of life we must face. However, like other parts of my life, I believe it's HOW we face it, how we continue to live; will ultimately influence and impact ourselves and others.

What has helped is to remind ourselves that time is limited. None of us knows when our last breath will be. Five minutes, tomorrow, next week, or ten years…we don't know. I choose to remember my mom (and loved ones) would want me to *LIVE* the life she could not, to the fullest. I am living through her and for her. I can wake up each day and *LOVE* my children, her grandchildren, our family, our friends, appreciate my life. I can try to *LEARN* something new every day, keep moving forward, keep experiencing new things, living the life I have been blessed with, to the fullest. I can *LISTEN* to my heart, hear her words, share the traditions, remember and share the memories. I chose to *LOOK* for and always try to focus on the POSITIVE; that although she is not here, I am. Remember there is **always** something positive if you choose to look for it.

Our time is limited, life is short, and my chapter needs to be too!! So, I will leave you with: hopefully an empty cup of coffee or tea, a new friend and email connection, anticipation of future impact stories, and "valuable visions" for "I", "F" and "E" in "Vallye's Valuable Visions on "LIFE" and a sincere and genuine wish for you. I hope even one thing, something, in this chapter has inspired you, made an impact, or influenced you to LOVE, LIVE, LEARN, LISTEN and LOOK for the positive in life and live your life to the very fullest.

ABOUT THE AUTHOR:

Social Media:

IG @etavelesolutions

FB @etavelesolutions

Email vallye@etavelesolutions.com

Vallye Adams is the founder and CEO of Etavele Solutions, LLC, a national consulting firm based in Tampa Florida. Unique like her name, Etavele offers solutions to 'elevate' and enhance events, engage boards, specialize in proven sustainable revenue development in the not-for-profit sector.

After attending the University of South Florida, Vallye's professional experience spans over twenty years, including multifamily property management, real estate sales, and over ten years in executive nonprofit management, fundraising, event development, expansion strategies, and new market growth.

Her "WOO" (*Winning other's Over*) strength and collaborative style has cultivated relationships, sponsorships, and corporate partnerships, paving the way for organizations around the country to *elevate* revenue and enhance event fundraising. Vallye's ability to help sail these vital "ships" has ensured elevated revenue growth to over $5 million in the last five years. Experience in expansion initiatives and new market growth in twenty-two states, Vallye focuses on grassroots efforts, building cohesive teams, motivated volunteers, and active structured boards.

Vallye believes actions speak louder than words and offers to personally help your organization make "the ask" and show you the $$! She is a licensed Florida auctioneer and emcee with the incredible team at Alpert Enterprises! She offers to consult and coach clients on cultivating exceptional events and or facilitate, manage and lead the revenue appeal from the frontlines.... the stage!

Now, a #1 International Best-Selling Author of, "YES I CAN!" 16 Success Secrets from Inspiring Women around the world, Vallye is honored to share her success secrets and energy on multiple podcasts, international publications, leadership series, and conferences. Proud to be an accomplished motivational trainer and public speaker, Vallye lives in Tampa with her husband of twenty-three years and three children. She enjoys tennis, traveling in their RV spending quality time in the mountains and beachside, and always loves learning, reading, and trying new things!

ABOUT THE LEAD AUTHOR

Chip Baker is a fourth-generation educator. He has been a teacher and coach for over twenty-two years. He is a multiple-time best-selling author, YouTuber, podcaster, motivational speaker, and life coach.

Chip Baker is the creator of the YouTube channel and podcast *Chip Baker—The Success Chronicles*, where he interviews people of all walks of life and shares their stories for positive inspiration and motivation.

Live. Learn. Serve. Inspire. Go get it!

Email: chipbakertsc@gmail.com
Online Store:
http://chip-baker-the-success-chronicles.square.site/
Facebook Page:
https://www.facebook.com/profile.php?id=100014641035295
Instagram: @chipbakertsc
LinkedIn:
http://linkedin.com/in/chip-baker-thesuccesschronicles-825887161
Twitter: @chipbaker19

Chip Baker—The Success Chronicles
YouTube: youtube.com/c/ChipBakerTheSuccessChronicles

Podcast: https://anchor.fm/chip-baker

Other Books:
Growing Through Your Go Through
Effective Conversation to Ignite Relationships
Suited for Success, Vol. 2
The Formula Chart for Life
The Impact of Influence Vol. 1 & 2
R.O.C.K. Solid
Stay on the Right Path

PICK UP THESE OTHER TITLES BY CHIP BAKER

 **GROWING THROUGH YOUR GO THROUGH**

 **EFFECTIVE CONVERSATION TO IGNITE RELATIONSHIP**

 **SUITED FOR SUCCESS: VOLUME 2**

 **THE FORMULA CHART FOR LIFE**

 **THE IMPACT OF INFLUENCE: VOLUME 1**

 **THE IMPACT OF INFLUENCE: VOLUME 2**

 **R.O.C.K. SOLID**

 **STAY ON THE RIGHT P.A.T.H.**

To order your autographed copies visit
http://chip-baker-the-success-chronicles.square.site/

Made in USA - Crawfordsville, IN
40870_9781737950134
03.23.2022 1636